More Praise for *Everyday Dad*

"*Everyday Dad* is an amazing true story that reads like a best-selling novel. Tim Delmont shares heart-warming and riveting true stories from his experience of suddenly being the sole parent of his ten-week-old daughter and five-year-old son after his wife's unexpected death. I fluctuated between tears and laughing out loud, retelling the unexpected funny stories. Tim's reflections on his experiences as a young dad, the support he received from family and friends, and the lessons he learned will make this a great choice for book clubs or families."

**—Donna Moores, principal gift officer,
  Greater Twin Cities United Way**

"Tim Delmont's account of single fatherhood is told with great honesty and increasing insight. He demonstrates the importance of reflection and meditative practice to make sense of the setbacks in life and gain clarity about which relationships are important to focus on, and how to develop and sustain them."

**—John von Knorring, president and founder,
  Stylus Publishing**

"Tim Delmont's story is filled with honest reflections as he copes with his grief, takes those first steps as a single parent, and sets out on a path of figuring out how best to care for his children. There are good lessons here for all parents on how to be present with and for one's children every day, no matter our circumstances."

**—Marie Kruskop, parent educator and coordinator of
  early childhood and family ministries,
  Westminster Presbyterian Church,
  Minneapolis**

Everyday Dad

A Memoir About Single Parenting

Tim Delmont

Mekenok Island Publishing
Minneapolis

Everyday Dad: A Memoir About Single Parenting
Published by Mekenok Island Publishing, Minneapolis, MN

Print ISBN: 979-8-9862233-0-8
E-book ISBN: 979-8-9862233-1-5
Audiobook ISBN: 979-8-9862233-2-2
Library of Congress Control Number 2022909105

Cover design by Jeenee Lee
Author photo by Tom Northenscold
Page design by Beth Wright, Wright for Writers LLC

Visit

www.aneverydaydad.org

to learn more about the author and being an everyday dad.

Contents

A gallery of photos precedes Chapter 29.

Preface

❁ ❁ ❁

My wife Sue died ten weeks after giving birth to our daughter. With little preparation, I became a single father of Anne and her five-year-old brother, Billy. In this book, I tell the story of our lives from 1976 through 1985, a decade in which I learned how to parent alone. I hope that this story offers insights about what a single father—or any father—of small children can do, if necessary. I hope, too, that the questions I raise about fathering will prompt men who read this book to act as what I will call everyday dads: dads who fully parent their children, share family responsibilities equally with their partners, and find balance among work, family, and other commitments.

I was in college when I first heard the spiritual "Sometimes I Feel like a Motherless Child." Its haunting lyrics about a child without a mother a long, long way from home stayed with me, a reminder of the need we have for a mother's love or the equivalent. I had no reason to anticipate that my children would lose their mother. When they did, I began a journey in which I tried to be both a mom and dad for them twenty-four hours a day. I struggled to answer the question "How do I fully replace their loving mother?" What I did, with what outcomes, is the story that follows.

In some respects, my story is unusual; there were far fewer single fathers with primary responsibility for raising children in the 1970s and early 1980s than there are today. But in other respects, my story is not exceptional at all. I know of many parents, single and otherwise, who have dealt with wrenching family crises precipitated by the death, absence, or

ix

illness of a loved one. However difficult their circumstances, they found ways to cope with their losses and manage their lives. Like them, much of the parenting I did without a partner involved trial and error. I made mistakes, but I can also point to successes.

This is a story about the challenges and joys I experienced during my initial ten years of single parenting. I remember this period fondly but ruefully, not fully certain what I might have done differently or better. I don't claim to represent all single fathers—others can speak for themselves. As I met single mothers and learned about their stories, I found we had similar as well as different experiences. I valued their insights.

Single parenting over a decade impacted me more than anything else ever has. It challenged me to reinvent myself as a father. It helped me clarify my values and priorities. And it informed my ongoing choices in career, marriage, and family life, for which I am grateful.

CHAPTER I

Beginnings

※ ※ ※

It was Easter Sunday in 1976 when our lives changed. Sue and I had resolved the problems that almost broke up our marriage. We had settled into a stable lifestyle with our son, Billy, and a new baby, Anne, in a new home and a new neighborhood. I liked my work, our marriage was strong, and we were overjoyed by the arrival of our daughter.

Sue and Billy and I started the day by looking for Easter eggs in our backyard. The winter snow had almost entirely melted, leaving clumps of wet, matted leaves piled around our tulip and daffodil patches, which had withstood another of Minnesota's hard winters. The grass was brown, some of it icy and slippery. As we searched for eggs hidden in the yard—some real, some plastic—our feet made tracks on the grass and in the muddy garden beds.

After a short time, Billy said, "I found three eggs, Dad, but I'm cold. Is it okay if I go inside to get warm?"

"Sure. That's a good idea. See you in a bit."

Sue and I looked at him as he ran across the lawn and up the back steps to our house. He seemed a blur of color: red tennis shoes, blue jeans, a blue jean jacket with the collar up, lots of brown hair flying, and a small smile on his face—just a sliver of white amid the blue, brown, and red. He was a happy child, spontaneous, curious, fond of artwork and football, a delight to be around.

After he went inside, the wind picked up. It cut through me and turned my hands red and swollen. The sky was dark and cloudy, and the air was cold—not a good day for the walks, bike rides, and cookouts we liked to do as a family.

"I think I'll call Daddy," Sue said. "I want to do it now in case he goes out for dinner." I nodded, and together we headed for the house, leaving the rest of the egg hunt for a later time.

The unseasonably cold weather kept us inside for the rest of the day. We colored more eggs, read stories together, and called family and friends to wish them a happy Easter. After lunch, I sat on the living room floor and played matchbox cars with Billy. The small, shiny army of many colors moved quickly to our touch.

Sue was in the rocking chair, gently holding ten-week-old Anne. A big baby at birth—nine pounds, fourteen ounces—she had come breech, requiring a C-section. As the weeks passed, Sue had grown stronger, her recovery on schedule, buoyed by the arrival of her little girl. Anne had a very round face, high cheekbones, and a small nose, all framed by tufts of red-blond hair. She carried tiny red birthmarks on her nose and cheeks, which would disappear in time. Except for her blue eyes, Anne was a mirror image of Sue, and others would invariably mention the striking resemblance when they saw her. When asked about Anne's looks, I usually said with a smile, "She has the good grace to look just like her mother."

Throughout these early months of Anne's life, Sue held her often, talked to her, nuzzled her, welcoming her to us and to her new home. When family and friends visited, she frequently refused to let them hold her. Anne was a gift, but not one to be fully shared with others.

That afternoon, after rocking the baby for a long time, Sue put her down for a nap in her cradle in our bedroom.

Later, I heard Sue's voice coming from the kitchen: "Daddy, you must come next week and stay with us for at least four or five days, maybe more." After hanging up the phone, she came into the living room. "He's going to come in ten days. Won't that be fun?"

"That's good news. We'll spoil Bob as best we can. Sort of like he did you."

"He should be so lucky." She smiled.

"I'll show Grandpa Bob all my cars and my posters, too," Billy said. Then he grabbed his jacket. "Can I go to Andy's now?"

"Yes—just watch when you cross the street."

We watched Billy go across the street to his friend Andy's house, then went to our bedroom to rest and, without having planned it, make love. With Sue's pregnancy and recovery from cesarean delivery, it had been a long time since we had been lovers. Afterward, we cuddled, Sue on her side, her back to me. When I got up to get a glass of water, she was quiet—asleep, it seemed. As I filled my glass at the kitchen sink, I heard Anne cry; she was awakening from her nap. I walked up the stairs to our bedroom.

Sue was still under the covers, with only the side of her face showing, the rest pressed into her pillow. Her face was an awful bluish-gray color I had never seen before, and her mouth and eyes were wide open but not moving. I cupped her face with both of my hands and said, "Sue, are you okay?" When she didn't respond, I pulled back the covers, shook her shoulders for a reaction, and put my ear to her chest to listen for a heartbeat. Out of the corner of my eye, I saw her upper arm extending from her nightgown, blue and still. I tipped her head back, put my mouth to hers, breathed quickly, listened for a breath, but nothing happened. When I pulled my mouth from hers, her head flopped listlessly onto the pillow.

I reached for the telephone next to the bedroom door and dialed 911.

"My wife is unconscious, maybe dead," I told the dispatcher. "Send help now." I gave our address. I could feel my heart beating faster, my breath was quick and short, my face was warm, and a sense of queasiness came over me. I'd never seen anyone whose skin color was blue. I didn't know what it meant.

Anne's cries broke through my thoughts. She could have been crying all the time I was upstairs. I didn't know; I hadn't heard her. I went to her and lifted her little body, snug in a pink sleeper, onto my chest and left shoulder, cradling her tiny, warm face against my cheek. She stopped whimpering and snuggled up to me, her hands—fingers curled together—resting in the crook of my neck. I held her tightly, patting her back.

Outside on the street, I could hear the horn of a fire truck blaring. Through our bedroom window, I saw the hook and ladder below, followed by a paramedic's van and a city police car. Doors flew open, and people in uniforms ran to my front door. Carrying Anne, I went into the hallway to the top of the stairs and yelled to them, "Come quickly, come quickly, we need you!"

The paramedics hurried into our bedroom. One gave Sue CPR, pressing down rhythmically on her chest with the palms of his hands. When nothing happened, they lifted her body and set it on the floor. I watched, holding Anne. The paramedics placed a pair of round black pads for a defibrillator on her chest and pressed the button that shocked her heart. She stayed inert, hardly moving. Her head lay flat against the floor, hair matted and pushed to one side.

The paramedics used the pads a second and a third time, but nothing happened. The paramedic turned toward me, a sad look on his face. He paused for a moment and said, "She's gone. There's nothing more we can do. I'm sorry." Sue lay on the bedroom floor in her rumpled nightgown, expressionless.

I heard his words, but they went right by me, disappearing in confusion. I couldn't make sense of what he had said. All I could think was *She's thirty-three. She's an athlete. She can't be dead.*

A police officer and several firefighters, in full black-and-yellow rubber suits and hats, stood in the hallway, peering into our bedroom. The firefighters looked at me, said nothing, and turned away. The police officer asked whether he could speak with me. As I left the bedroom, I saw a paramedic reach into a black bag, pulling out what looked like a large olive-green duffel bag with a long zipper on it.

I don't remember going down the steps or into the dining room. I do remember walking in a continuous circle around our dining room table, patting Anne's back and responding to the officer's questions: "When did this happen, Mr. Delmont? What were you doing? How did your wife die? What do you think caused her death?"

Then I stopped walking and turned toward the stairway. I saw the paramedics struggling with the green bag they carried between them. *What are they doing?* I thought. *Why do they have that bag?* A sick feeling spread through me.

I was aware of the officer still talking to me and of something that sounded like a truck noise outside, but the sounds and images swept by me, as if I were free-falling, out of control. The only thing I could see in vivid detail was the green bag, with bulges distending its sides. *Sue is in that bag. They're taking her away.*

In my mind, I saw her in her white wedding dress, standing next to me under the apple tree in her parents' backyard where we were married. I saw her pushing our son's head out of her birth canal, sweating and crying. I saw her as we stood together at our kitchen sink, doing dishes, her head back as she laughed and said, "You're really funny. I didn't know that about you when we got married, but you make me laugh. What a wonderful surprise."

I was stunned and confused. Helpless. It was as if kidnappers had come into our house and taken Sue and I couldn't do anything about it. I wanted to stop the paramedics—make them drop the bag she was in. That made no sense, but neither did her death. The paramedics went past me, out the front door, down the steps, onto the boulevard, and were gone. I felt like crying, but I couldn't. My heart beat very fast.

I turned my head when the officer said, "Did you and your wife get along well? If not, will you tell me about it?"

Why doesn't he leave like the others? I thought.

Then it dawned on me that *I* was a suspect. He thought I might have killed her. Now I felt tears in the corners of my eyes and my lips began to quiver. I managed a half smile, realizing how ridiculous the situation was. *It's not enough that she's gone, but I need an alibi.* I didn't, couldn't, say anything. The officer warned me to stay in the city. He said Sue's body would be at the county medical examiner's office, and I should call them if I had any questions.

I walked outside with the officer. He slowly drove away with red lights still flashing. I first looked at his car and then saw my neighbors—perhaps twenty or more—standing quietly on the boulevard in front of our house and across the street, waiting, some with arms folded, watching me. I didn't know what to say to them, so I said nothing. I turned around and walked back into our house to call Ad, Sue's stepfather, and Irene, her mother, to tell them that their only daughter had died.

"Ad, I have to tell you something terrible. Sue has just died, maybe from a heart attack. I don't know for sure. Please come over. I need your help. I'll tell you more when you get here."

Ad said he'd be right over. He'd have to come alone—Irene was out of town.

While waiting for his arrival, I fed Anne her bottle, sitting in the rocking chair. I was in a daze. I could feel Anne's compact little body nestled in my arms and on my legs as she sucked on the nipple. I closed my eyes and saw the two of us being swept up, tumbling around like Dorothy's house in *The Wizard of Oz*.

When Ad arrived, I gave Anne to him.

"I have to get Billy," I told him. "He's with Andy."

I found Billy standing behind a tree in front of Andy's house.

"I was coming home, but I saw the fire engine and police car, and all those guys running around. I was scared," he said.

I took his hand. "Billy, we need to talk by ourselves, away from others."

We walked a short distance to the corner of the block. I knelt on one leg, my face close to his, my hands on his sides. I felt numb as I tried to find the words to tell him his mother was dead.

"Billy, Mommy's heart stopped beating. The paramedic people in the blue clothes tried to start it again, but it wouldn't work anymore. Mommy's dead, Billy. She's gone from us and can't ever come back." Billy looked surprised and frightened. He reached for me, putting his arms around my neck. I picked him up and held him, his head moving to my shoulder. For a while we hugged without talking, locked together, under the gray sky.

Then he lifted his head. "Will I ever have a mommy again?"

"Someday," I said.

Billy and I walked to our house, hand in hand, past the fire engine and a few of my neighbors, who were talking to each other. As we walked up the steps to our house, I wondered whether something else unexpected was going to happen.

I asked Ad to stay with Billy so that I could go back outside. I was having trouble breathing; I felt like there was a force, a pressure pushing on me, especially around my head and upper body. I needed to relieve the pressure, to have some time to myself. I walked the short distance to a nearby park—up a hill, across it, and down toward a clump of trees, some birch, some walnut, all swaying and bending under the late afternoon wind. It was still cloudy and cold. I stopped and looked up. Words tumbled out: "We were happy again. How could you go away? How could you do this?"

At that moment, a sharp pain ran from my right shoulder to my stomach, as if someone had cut me inside with a shard of glass. I took a quick breath and felt the pain again, longer this time. Doubling over, I wrapped both arms around my middle, holding myself in place. Then the pain went away. I walked past the trees, up the hill, and home. The pressure was gone. My mind cleared, and questions came: *Who do we tell about Sue's death? What do Anne and Billy need? What do I do next?*

Ad and I put Billy and Anne in the car and drove to his house. We spoke little on the way, thinking about whom to call with the terrible news.

After dinner, Billy walked up to me, tugged at my shirt sleeve, and said, "Dad, I think Anne's hungry. She's making these weird sounds that are bugging me. Can you do something?"

"Sure, Billy. I'll get her bottle and then we'll read a story. Okay?" He nodded and headed for the living room, where Ad had lit a fire. I warmed Anne's bottle, fed her, and put her to bed.

I went into the bedroom where Billy and I would sleep. Ad had helped him wash up and get into his pajamas. He was waiting for me, under the covers, book in hand. Once he was asleep, I made a drink and told Ad everything that had happened, from the Easter egg hunt to when I picked up Billy.

"It's unbelievable. Irene and I will help you, Tim. Anything," Ad said quietly, leaning toward me. I nodded without speaking. I could feel tears forming in my eyes. I was so grateful for his kindness.

We made phone calls to our family and friends. Ad made the most difficult call, to Irene. She was in New York City, spending the Easter weekend with old friends. Just before she left on her trip, she and Sue had had an explosive, shouting argument—not unusual, but hurtful to both of them.

"You've been drinking again, haven't you?" Irene had said.

"No, I haven't. I'm perfectly fine," Sue retorted.

"You're not. Are you ever going to get over this stuff? It's sickening."

"You can't talk to me that way, especially when I'm fine. I want you to leave now."

Irene had grabbed her coat and hat and left without another word. The next day, Sue had apologized, but Irene had refused to accept the apology.

After Ad called her and told her the news, Irene immediately booked a ticket home. She spent the night in Chicago's O'Hare Airport, alone and fully awake, watching one janitor and then another do their work. Later she told me that she remembered her life with Sue as she waited for her early morning flight to Minneapolis. After she returned, she showed me a picture of Sue, age six, running on a sunny beach in Honolulu, blond hair flying, with a big smile, free and happy. "That's my Sue," she said, pulling the picture to her chest.

That night I couldn't fall asleep. I remembered making love with Sue and realized that as we finished, she had likely had a heart attack. But I hadn't sensed it at all when it happened. How could I have missed it? How was that even possible? I felt confused and stupid. "How can you not know that your wife is dying in your arms?" would become a recurring question for me. I was embarrassed that I hadn't understood what was happening or done enough to save her. We might have gotten help sooner if I had been more attentive after we had made love or if I had stayed in bed with her longer or if I had taken less time to get a drink or, for that matter, if we had not made love at all. I didn't feel guilty, but I did feel that I had failed her.

The memories of how she died—and of the actions of the paramedics, the firefighters, the police, and the rest—stayed with me in the months that followed, always vivid and intense. They would come back at nighttime and in other quiet moments, gnawing away at me. Sometimes I recalled everything in detail, but just as often I repressed the images and my feelings so that I could try to sleep or take care of things that needed to be done.

On the nightstand at Ad and Irene's the night of Sue's death was a copy of the biography *Papa Hemingway*. I had started to read it during a visit we had made there a few weeks earlier. I opened the book, paged through it, and saw, at the beginning of chapter 5, a quote from Hemingway's *A Moveable Feast*:

You expected to be sad in the fall. Part of you died each year when the leaves fell from the trees and their branches were bare against the wind and the cold, wintry light. But you knew there would always be the spring, as you knew the river would flow again after it was frozen. When the cold rains kept on and killed the spring, it was as though a young person had died for no reason.

CHAPTER 2

Sue

✄ ✄ ✄

The first time I saw Sue, she was driving a white convertible with red upholstery, the top down. She had a colorful headband in her hair and large sunglasses on; she seemed affluent and accomplished. *Who's that? I'd love to meet her*, I thought. A few weeks later, in a graduate class at the University of Minnesota, she walked into the room. After class, we began a conversation. We were both enrolled in a master's degree program in social work: she was preparing to be a family counselor, and I wanted to work as a counselor with adolescent boys.

She was classy—very poised and pretty, blond, with brown eyes. I learned that she was athletic: a swimmer, diver, skier, and tennis player. Along with her mother, she performed in theater productions. She was friendly and confident.

During the first year of graduate school, she was involved with another guy. But one day in the fall of the second year, I took a chance. I stopped my car near a public pay phone and gave her a call to ask whether she was still seeing the guy. She said that she'd broken up with her boyfriend in the middle of summer. I told her that I had really enjoyed our earlier conversation and asked whether we could have lunch on campus in the next couple of weeks.

"You know, I'd like that," she said in a friendly way. We picked a date, and I hung up the phone. *Wow, how lucky is that?* I thought. I felt great.

We started dating: movies, picnics, bike rides, visits to museums, dinners at her place or mine. All were easy. The more time we spent together, the more I wanted to be with her. She was curious, creative, and fun, with a rare awareness and empathy.

I remember a time when we saw each other after being apart for months. I had driven back to Minnesota from Florida, where I had been working. When she opened her apartment door, she was dressed in an orange and light blue Hawaiian muumuu and had a white orchid in her hair. She looked tanned and lovely. Her apartment was filled with dozens of small lighted candles on tables, bureaus, and bookshelves. Yellow marigolds and white daisies were in vases everywhere. Folk music was playing. I was enchanted.

After a year and half of dating, we decided to get married. My proposal was casual—over a dinner. "Well," she said, "quite a production!" Both of us laughed. She said yes. We went shopping the next day for our wedding rings and picked them out together.

The first years of our marriage were fun, whether it was just the two of us or we were spending time with friends and family. We started our professional careers. We were thrilled when she got pregnant and when Billy was born. But things went badly after his birth.

During her maternity leave, Sue was laid off. Finding another position as a social worker would be difficult, even unlikely. Meanwhile, I had quit my job for what I thought was a better one. I'd received a job offer, which I accepted, but two weeks before I was to start, the offer was rescinded.

We were both shocked and scared, unsure of what to do and what was to come. While applying for professional jobs, I took a low-paying position assembling farm machinery, which a friend had offered me. My outdoor work site was next to an office building in which I had previously worked. More than once, I caught former colleagues of mine staring out their windows at me. I kept working, too embarrassed to acknowledge them.

For Sue, the early months of my underemployment and the loss of her own job took a toll we hadn't expected. In the first summer after Billy's birth, she became depressed, moody, anxious, and discouraged about herself and our future as a couple. She started drinking more and more. Usually tastefully dressed, she now sometimes stayed in her bathrobe all day, hair undone. I found empty liquor bottles tucked in umbrella stands, covered by caps and scarves, and hidden under our bed or in our closets.

After I found a better-paying white-collar job, she would call me at my office, but her messages made little sense. Sometimes I left work early during the day to check on her and Billy, using vacation hours for longer stretches. On occasion, she accused me of having affairs, especially with a very beautiful former student of mine from when I was a high school teacher, who had been a favorite of ours.

"Are you seeing her?" she asked frequently.

"I'm not, and I'm not going to," I told her.

Despite our difficulties, we were still able to talk about her earlier painful family experiences. For three and a half years during World War II, her father, Bob, was a soldier stationed in New Guinea, with almost no visits home. After the war, he and Irene tried to rebuild their marriage but failed. A separation and divorce followed. During this time, Bob saw Sue on Saturdays. Once the divorce was finalized, he moved to California, and his visits to Sue, who was now five, were limited to one month a year, a condition of his and Irene's divorce decree.

"I just couldn't stand dropping her off at Irene's, after my Saturday visits," Bob later told me. "Sue cried and cried and sometimes clung to my legs. I had to leave Minneapolis."

When Irene remarried, she left Sue—age six—with her grandmother Hazel in Minneapolis and went to live with her new husband in Omaha. She had married a man who wanted no children in his life, hers or theirs. When he died unexpectedly six months later, Sue was reunited with her mother. But the abandonment by both biological parents had hurt her badly. She missed both of them and didn't understand why she couldn't see them more often.

"Grandma Haz was good to me," she told me once. "I loved working with her on her big garden and having all her cats around. But I remember looking out her living room windows to see if Mother or Daddy was coming, but they didn't. It hurt a lot."

She remembered that in her middle school and high school years, her mother was unpredictable, sometimes caring and sometimes hostile and rejecting. Although Sue was talented, attractive, and successful in school, she rarely knew how she would be treated at home. She became unsure of herself, and that self-doubt reappeared after we lost our jobs.

In our talks, I learned things about her that I hadn't fully known, which helped me understand her better. The confident, vivacious woman I had fallen in love with and married had a complicated, often destructive family history.

This stew of present and past losses was debilitating to her. She started abusing pills: uppers to get through the day and downers to get to sleep, which then required more uppers to keep the cycle going. She used her keen intelligence to persuade doctors in different clinics to prescribe what she wanted. I was no match for her wits, and giving up her checkbook and credit cards hardly slowed her down.

Her parents and some close friends saw the changes, too, and urged me to do something. With financial help from her parents, Sue and I got marital counseling. It wasn't easy finding the best fit for us. We tried one psychiatrist, then a second, before discovering a family therapist who helped us deal with our conflicts more respectfully. We also went to Alcoholics Anonymous and Al-Anon meetings.

As the months and then years went on, we still had good times together. And Sue found work, which also helped. She was hired for part-time social work jobs in a Minneapolis junior high school, a nursing home, and a human services office.

I remember tender moments between us. Once I made her a long wooden flower box, painted blue, which I hung on a wall by the outdoor patio of our apartment. After I had mounted it and filled it with bright yellow daffodils and daises, which she could see through our kitchen window, she came outside and pulled my hand to her cheek. She had tears in her eyes and, with a shy smile, said, "Thank you, honey. I love it." Many times, we took Billy to one of the nearby city parks or lakes for a picnic supper. We both wanted a good life for our little boy, and we felt united in our hope for him.

Despite her progress and our own contented moments together, we had frequent arguments over money, her drinking, and our roles as parents.

"For God's sake, why can't you get over this?" I'd say in anger.

"What do you know about it?" she'd respond. On at least one occasion, Billy was in the room and heard us. After about two years of stagnation, we agreed to separate.

I made the decision to leave only after giving it a lot of thought. I knew I had to separate from Sue, to get distance from her. I was frustrated with our life together and felt like a failure. It didn't seem that anything I was doing as a husband made a significant difference. I didn't know whether I was promoting or enabling some of her behaviors or whether I had the skills and attitudes that could help her meet her needs and strengthen our relationship. Her alcohol and drug abuse masked deeper pain, but I didn't know what I could do to help her find her way out. I wasn't prepared to deal effectively with our problems.

Sometimes I felt shell-shocked, incompetent—like someone who had fallen into Alice's rabbit hole, swirling around and around, dropping farther with each spin. Our therapy had helped us relate better to each other but hadn't seemed to resolve the deeper issues that were undermining our marriage. I felt confused and needed time away.

I was hesitant to leave Billy with Sue. Would he be safe with her? Before leaving, I talked with our therapist, Sue's parents, and a few relatives and friends. They reassured me that Sue could handle it. We thought her love for Billy and her commitment to his welfare would carry through, that his needs would draw out her most nurturing, conscientious behavior. There was no evidence that she had ever neglected or abused Billy. I also thought that if I took Billy from her when I left, it could lead to a court battle over his custody. In that era, family courts almost universally supported the mother's rights over the father's rights in divorce and child custody cases. The pendulum had not yet swung; joint custody was nearly unknown.

While I knew separation might lead to divorce, I hoped that my leaving might motivate Sue to better control her alcohol and drug use, which was already significantly lessening, and lead to a renewal of our relationship.

I rented a small apartment near the University of Minnesota, where, after four months of working part-time, I had found a full-time position. The higher salary of my new job enabled me to meet the expenses of our two homes. I was a five-minute drive from Sue and Billy. I talked with them almost every night, visited regularly, and spent time with Billy when Sue went out. The separation did help me; at least I slept better and exercised more. I wasn't sure, though, how much I loved Sue and how much I wanted to work on our marriage. Divorce was still an option.

While I recognized that my attitudes and behaviors were contributing to our estrangement, I saw our marriage problems chiefly as her problems, not believing that I had as much work to do as she did. When our therapist suggested that he see Sue exclusively and didn't recommend continuing therapy for us as a couple or for me separately, I took that as additional evidence that our marriage problems were more hers than mine.

While apart from Sue, I spent time with Connie, the former student Sue had asked me about. She was beautiful and had enormous warmth, a dazzling smile, insight and empathy about children, and at least some interest in me. I made dinner for her once at my apartment, thinking we might have a future if my marriage ended. I knew that by dating her, I wasn't focusing exclusively on repairing my relationship with Sue, which should have been my priority. I felt guilty but didn't stop reaching out to Connie. She was dating another guy at the time, though, and, after a while, knew what was best for both of us.

"Go back to your wife," she said.

Several months after Sue and I separated, we both had our respective Alcoholics Anonymous meetings on the same evening and in the same building. Afterward, as we walked to our cars, she stopped and turned her head slightly to me as she said, "I am losing everything I love: my husband, my son, my job, my life."

After that, she changed her behavior dramatically. She redecorated our apartment, reached out more to friends, and, on many occasions, invited me to dinner. She stopped using drugs completely and limited herself to a glass of wine at dinner. Surprisingly, she didn't experience withdrawal symptoms—a relief for both of us.

We rebuilt our friendship by spending time with Billy and "dating" again—movies, plays, and museum visits were favorites. We rekindled some of the joy we had originally discovered in each other and, after six months of our trial separation, decided to reunite.

Within a year, we had rebuilt our relationship, fully shared the parenting of Billy, and were on solid ground financially. I was enrolled in the last required classes for my PhD in educational policy and administration, and she explored admission to a PhD program in family social science. We decided to have a second child. Within a month of trying, Sue was pregnant with Anne. We were both ecstatic.

It remained a mystery to me how Sue had managed to get better. Therapy and AA may have helped. She also got support from family and friends. The separation might have been a factor, too.

I knew that whatever I had to offer her came with limitations. I didn't know that much more about how to be a husband or a father. I did know that she loved me and wanted us to parent our children together. After our reunion, she told me, "When we got married, I didn't love you intensely; now I do." Sue was brave. Somehow, she had pulled herself out of a spiraling fall. She found hope and shared it with me, helping us build a new life together with our children.

CHAPTER 3

The Memorial Service

Ad, Irene, and I planned the memorial service for Sue at a local Unitarian Universalist church. Irene and I would speak, as would a friend of the family. Cindy, Sue's sister-in-law, an accomplished organist, would provide music. Irene volunteered to pull the service program together and have it printed. Knowing the shock and sorrow Sue's family and friends would feel at the death of someone so young, we tried hard to prepare messages that would offer some kind of hope. We knew, however, that the service would not be the celebration of life often associated with the death of a much older loved one.

One night when I was putting Billy to bed, his favorite worn, torn white blankie in hand, he said, "It's just like Mommy went to the store—only she'll never come back." He was starting to understand what it meant that his mom had died.

A few days before the service, Bob, Sue's father, arrived from California. Bob and Billy resembled each other: brown hair, brown eyes, compact features, handsome faces. A champion college and city tennis player, Bob moved lightly, with an easy smile. Billy and I were glad to see him and have him stay at our house. Anne was at Ad and Irene's.

Bob told me that when he heard the news from my father that Sue had died, he was incredulous: "My Sue died? I just spoke with her this morning. We had a lovely talk. She was fine. It can't be." Later, he found himself crying, stumbling around his apartment. He saw a small dirt spot on his kitchen floor and was suddenly driven to scrub the entire floor on his hands and knees, pushing the hand sponge over and over, water sloshing about.

I kept Billy out of school so we could see how he was doing. The first day Bob was with us, he walked Billy to our nearby convenience store. Without warning, he said to the clerk, "This boy has just lost his mother." The clerk nodded and rang up the sale. Like all of us, Bob was in shock, not quite knowing what to say.

Through the first week, more than a hundred condolence cards and notes arrived from around the world. People who had met Sue at every age of her life remembered her. As a child, she had lived with her mother in Hawaii for six years. As a teenager, she had been an exchange student in Belgium. During college, she had participated in Minnesota senator Hubert Humphrey's campaign for vice president and attended the Democratic National Convention. After college, she had worked as a researcher on child development issues in a London social service agency. Family members and friends saw her as a genuine, open person, someone of unusual intelligence and sensitivity, someone to whom they felt close no matter how long ago they had seen her.

An aunt, who had known her from birth, wrote in a note titled "Things I will never forget about Sue":

> Her sincere interest in whoever she was with—the warm
> way she greeted us as if it was important to her. She liked
> to talk to people—to get beneath the surface. She was an
> in-depth person—always recommending a book she had
> read, a place to visit, a record to enjoy. She looked at us
> when she talked to us—she observed changes, she sensed
> feelings. She put first things first: her husband and chil-
> dren, people who mattered to her, then things.

These were qualities that I loved about her, too. When I thought about our children now, I had a bleak feeling. Billy and Anne would never really know their mother and would always have to live with the mystery of her death.

One afternoon, Bob took Billy for a walk. When they came back, he told me that Billy had looked hard at him and asked, "What will happen to me if Daddy dies, too?" Bob had explained that he and Granny Irene and Grandpa Ad and Nana (my mother) would always take care of him, but that Daddy was strong and healthy and would be there for him. As I went upstairs to sleep that night, I wondered: How would Sue's death change Billy's life? How could I help him? And Anne, too—what was ahead for her? What kind of fathering would she need? I felt unsure and anxious about our future.

We had a wake the day before the memorial service. We gave Billy the choice of whether to go; initially undecided, he said he wanted to come— "to see my dead Mommy." In the parking lot, he changed his mind, choosing instead to stay in the car with an adult friend. Bob and I left him in the car and began walking toward the mortuary when we heard his voice: "Daddy, take me with you." He opened the car door and ran to us.

Inside the building, I picked him up and held him as we walked to the casket, which was across the room. I told him that Mommy was in the box and was not alive anymore, and that we were going to look at her one last time. He nodded. We stood at the casket together, looking down at Sue. Seeing Sue as a corpse—waxy, dressed for the cemetery—stunned me. Billy looked intently at his mother but said nothing.

As he and I turned to go, my grandfather Nick, who was behind us in line, said to me, "This is a terrible thing, Timmy, losing your young wife. But these little ones will give you back your life." I had no idea what he was talking about, what was ahead, but found his comment comforting anyway. He knew more about life than I did. He had had a difficult first marriage with a wife who had also been an alcoholic—my father's moth- er—and a second marriage, with three children, that was succeeding. At nearly ninety he had the long view, too, and maybe he would be right.

Bob, Billy, and I drove home in silence. When we stopped in our drive- way, Billy finally spoke.

"That wasn't Mommy. That was a dummy. Can I go play with Andy now?" he asked. I nodded and smiled a little at how he was able to switch gears. He grabbed his race cars off the back porch and ran down the drive- way and across the street to see Andy, who was waiting on the curb for him.

The next day, First Universalist Church was filled when I walked up the center aisle to the front of the chapel. I held Billy's hand and carried

Anne in a travel seat, which I set on the floor next to us. Irene had dressed her in pink, and she had a small rattle in her hand. She was alert and almost smiling. Billy climbed into my lap.

After an introduction by the minister and a Bach passage by Cindy, a family friend read Irene's tribute—she had decided not to do it herself. Sue, Irene wrote, "was a victim of all the worst uncertainties and insecurities of the World War II period: geographical separations from those she loved, painful goodbyes, death of a stepfather, and more." But she created "deep, close, touching relationships . . . and did not let people go."

She closed with these words:

> There is no way of passing on all the things that Sue gave me, but I feel a responsibility to try to live by—for the rest of my life—and impart to others as least one of her gifts: Pay attention. Be aware. Touch each other. Look at your baby, your husband, your friend! Listen! Hear! Don't hold back. Don't put it off. There is truly never enough time.

Gisela, the second speaker, gave many examples of Sue as "a giving person," described her as "beauty, color, and life," and reminded us that "it is perhaps good for all of us who mourn for her to know that she left us at a time when she was truly happy. Almost the last words I heard her say were 'It is so good to know that really, here is the pot of gold: Tim's love, my two children, everything.'"

When I got up to speak, I was dry-mouthed, weak, and tired. The mood in the room was somber. Some people were crying softly or sniffling; others—many of whom I knew well—sat expressionless. It was almost too much. In composing my remarks, I had tried to find a way to introduce some lightness or humor through a story or anecdote, reflecting the joyfulness that Sue brought to our lives, but I couldn't find a way to do it, and I didn't when I spoke.

I talked about how Sue had given me insight into how people may treat each other in the "day by day" as well as intimate experiences of life. She had stressed how important it was to listen to other people, really listen, to better understand their needs and ideas. As a social worker, Sue was trained to listen carefully to her clients, but I hadn't thought about how important listening was in daily life until she and I talked about it. A simple insight, but one I had overlooked.

I mentioned that in our marriage service, she and I had said about our home, "Let there be a spirit of gentleness, generosity, hospitality, and acceptance for all who come. Let it be a place where children are nurtured well." We both believed in these ideas and had tried to live them during our marriage.

These were my final words:

> With Sue gone, I truly need your help in caring for, directing, and enriching our children's lives. I know, too, that to be the kind of father I want to be, I will also need your understanding, your time, perhaps your criticisms, and your friendship. For I believe, as Pastor John Cummins of this church has written, that "In the end every one of us will die, will lose everything he loves, his possessions, his dear ones, even his life. We must reach out and hold and comfort one another while we can." Sue did these things. I'll try.

That night I was awake for hours, thinking of Sue. Before I fell asleep, I reread a note that her aunt Garneth had sent me, with a poem:

> The tide recedes
> but leaves behind
> bright seashells on
> the sand.
> The sun goes down
> but gentle warmth
> still lingers in the land.
> The music stops
> and yet it echoes on
> in sweet refrain.
> For every joy that passes
> something beautiful remains.

I put Garn's note on my nightstand and kept it there for a long, long time. I liked remembering the good times with Sue, especially the many moments with our children. But I felt sad and discouraged that, after all the work we had done to rebuild our marriage, she was gone. And her own losses were incalculable: no more time with her children, her husband, her family and friends, her work, the life she could have lived. For me, her death created a void that would never fully go away. It was so cruel and stupid.

I wished, too, that I could have said goodbye to her. Decades later, I was able to say goodbye to my mother and to Irene. I sat next to each one, holding their hands, frail and light. Their breathing slowed and became labored, their mouths open, faces expressionless, as death came to them. I knew, though, that they were still within reach. I communicated with them. I told them that I loved them, and I thanked them for what they brought to my life and to the lives of Billy and Anne. Sue's death, so sudden and unexpected, was different. There was no farewell for her or for us. There was, however, a legacy.

In the first weeks after her death, I didn't realize that she had left me anything I could build my life on as a single parent. It was over the years that I learned to appreciate what our time together had taught me. Having survived losing her, I knew in my life after that, no matter how hard things got, the problems of the moment were not as significant as they appeared nor without possible remedy. I had my two children and my life. That attitude helped me respond to family problems and stresses calmly, taking things in stride. Many times, I thought, *We can get through this— nobody's going to die.* And I knew her family was there for the kids and me as well.

Sue had told me how much she appreciated me and what I did for our family and our life together. That gave me confidence that I could succeed as a single father. The positive impact she had on me during her life and after her death was enormous and lasting.

After the memorial service, Bob left for his home in Los Angeles. We agreed that in August we would meet in Ocean Park, Maine, a small seaside town. Bob had grown up in Maine and had spent parts of summers in Ocean Park with Sue and other family members. Sue had told me once that she wished to be cremated and have her ashes spread along the beach-front there, where she said she had been her happiest. Bob would make the arrangements for us to stay at the family cottage and investigate plane rentals. He thought that distributing her ashes by plane rather than in a walk along the beach would be a better approach in the crowded summer season. Billy and I would join him, and I would bring Sue's ashes.

It was easy to see why Sue had loved her father—he was kind, thoughtful, funny, and caring. In time, he would become a very good friend of mine and a positive influence in my children's lives.

CHAPTER 4

Questions with No Answers

✳ ✳ ✳

In the middle of June, the county medical examiner's office sent me Sue's certificate of death. I made an appointment with her doctor to discuss the certificate, which stated that she died of "cardiac arrhythmia of undetermined origin." I didn't understand what that meant.

"We can't explain what caused her death," her doctor said. "There are some new studies of mothers who had an imbalance in body chemistry, as she did, who died from cardiac arrhythmia following childbirth. Too high or too low a concentration of minerals is a risk factor. But we don't know if this was a significant contributing factor or not."

"Was her weight a factor? I think she had gained about fifty pounds during her pregnancy."

"Possibly, but again, we can't be certain. Many mothers gain that much and don't die. She had toxemia, too, which pushed up her blood pressure some and contributed to her weight gain. That's why we had her take it easy—and stay in bed the last weeks. But we don't know if her toxemia was a real risk factor."

"We made love just before she died. Was that a factor?"

"No, it is very unlikely; she was healthy enough for sex. Addiction to drugs or alcohol is a risk factor for arrhythmia, but she didn't have any of them in her system. We just don't know what killed her or under what other circumstances she might have died. Or when. It could have happened at any time or never. I am afraid the cause of her death is a mystery."

I felt frustrated and irritated. Couldn't there be some kind of answer?

"How quickly did she die?"

"Probably within a few minutes or even less. Something caused her heart to beat very erratically, which prevented it from pumping blood effectively to her brain and it shut down. By the time you found her, and certainly by the time the paramedics tried CPR and defibrillation, she couldn't be revived. Her brain cells had died in the first few minutes after the arrhythmia, and skin color can change that quickly, too."

After I talked with the doctor, I didn't feel any better. Neither did any of the family members with whom I shared the news. A definitive explanation might have filled the void. I was relieved that our lovemaking apparently did not contribute to her death, although I still wondered whether that was true. It was hard to shake the feeling that I should have done something to prevent her death.

CHAPTER 5

The New Normal

❂ ❂ ❂

Following the memorial service and Bob's departure, it began to sink in that I was a single father of a five-year-old and a baby, with a job. My first priority was to find childcare.

My initial search was fruitless. Professional babysitting agencies provided no more than eight service hours per day and would not place a nanny in a permanent position. Licensed daycare facilities would not take a two-month-old child. City and county social service agencies did not provide live-in daycare services. Many childcare programs couldn't meet our needs: the distance between our home and the institution was too great; enrollment limits had been set, and some were overcrowded; and my new salary exceeded the maximum income allowed.

In the first months, I found help at home for Anne during my working hours from her grandmothers, an aunt, my neighbors, and college-age babysitters. I drove Billy to school, and he took the bus home or to neighbors' houses. Help came to us and we went to it. While scrambling week to week, I placed ads for a long-term nanny in the *Minneapolis Tribune*, the *Minnesota Daily* (the University of Minnesota student newspaper), our local neighborhood papers, and employment offices, churches, and neighborhood co-ops. Ads in the *Tribune* produced the best results.

Irene screened the callers, together we selected the most promising candidates, and I interviewed them. Most were middle-age single women, usually divorced, whose children were young adults. Some were retirees, often widows seeking a more active life. A few were teenage or college-age women, either under- or unemployed, with children. One young moth-er brought her six-month-old infant to the interview. Through April and May and into June, I didn't find anyone I wanted to hire.

While we made the makeshift system work—and I was grateful for the steady stream of volunteer help—I was discouraged and exhausted. The list of tasks seemed endless: get the kids ready for the day; drop them off and pick them up; go grocery shopping; make the meals; wash, dry, and iron the clothes; take care of the house, garage, car, and yard needs; stay in touch with the family and caregivers; pay the bills; avoid sickness; go to work and try to do my job; put the kids to bed; make and keep the pe-diatrician, dentist, and doctor appointments; and the pièce de résistance: survive Anne's 11:00 p.m., 2:00 a.m., and 6:00 a.m. feedings. The days and nights blurred together, driven by a predictable to-do list, but I never quite knew when something unexpected would undermine the makeshift schedule we had created. I kept thinking, *Can I do this? For how long?* And I wondered, *How long will I feel sad about Sue's death?* Feeling this way was so discouraging, so tiring.

When a family member stayed overnight to tend to the kids, I was grateful for a full night's sleep. If possible, I would also help my cause by taking an afternoon nap during a work break. At my job, employees had fifteen-minute morning and afternoon breaks and thirty minutes for lunch. With my supervisor's okay, I merged my two shorter breaks into a thirty-minute slot in the afternoon, typically at 3:00, when the effects of the nighttime feedings were slowing me down. In the university's student center, there was a room near the faculty library called the quiet room that had twelve twin beds, six to a side. It had been created chiefly as a resting spot for elderly faculty and staff who continued to work in campus offices after their retirements. Aside from occasional snores from nappers, it was blissfully still and quiet. I loved that twenty-five- to thirty-minute break and knew that I was lucky to have it.

In time, I saw Anne's nighttime feedings as a gift rather than a nui-sance. I had fed Anne regularly before Sue's death, too; Sue was under doctor's orders to rest as much as possible to recover from her surgery and allow her milk supply to build, so I was the one who got up. It was differ-ent now. Every day, there was so much more to do. But as time went on, I resented the feedings less, concentrating more on Anne—so tiny, so fragile, so hungry! It felt good to hold her little body in the crook of my arm during feedings. My feelings of irritation changed to expectation: Have I warmed the milk just right? Will she take it all? Has she been burped enough? Will she go back to sleep? It was almost a game, a competition I wanted to win.

There were lighter moments, too. Sometimes I played music to soothe both of us during the nighttime feedings. A favorite of mine was James Taylor's second album and its popular title song, the lullaby "Sweet Baby James." When it played, I'd hold baby Anne on my left shoulder and do an awkward waltz to the music while mouthing the lyrics. On some occasions, I felt her little body moving to the music. I loved that.

Sue and I had brought this baby into the world. We owed her everything we could do to start her life right. One night, I looked into her eyes as she drank from the bottle, dropping my face closer to hers, and said, "Hello little darling. You didn't decide to show up. You had nothing to do with it. But I promise to be your daddy, to be there for you always." At that exact moment she spit the nipple from her lips, stopped wiggling, and looked right at me, the hint of a smile on her face. It was a moment of connection—unscripted and real.

Before Anne was born, when there was just Billy, Sue and I shared many parenting duties. I often gave him his bottle at night and bathed, fed, and dressed him. I read him stories, played games with him, and took him with me shopping for groceries, clothes, and household goods. We went on outings to parks and playgrounds. I took him to the doctor. Everyday stuff. But now I had a baby and a small child to raise on my own. I was 100 percent responsible for meeting their needs.

I got good advice from family members, neighbors, and friends, some of whom recommended books. I reread parts of Dr. Spock's *Baby and Child Care*, which encouraged parents to build trusting relationships through engaging, talking with, and touching their children, and Rudolf Dreikurs's *Children: The Challenge*, in which Dreikurs said that children need a "feeling of belonging" and a sense of community to develop a healthy personality.

Following Sue's example, I often held and rocked Anne during bottle feeding and before naps and bedtime. Changing her diapers and dressing her were times for touching, talking, making faces. When I made our meals, I put her in a travel seat on the kitchen counter so I could look at her and talk to her. We almost always followed each other with our eyes.

I learned new things about taking care of babies. That real Pampers were far more durable than the cheaper store brands available at pharmacies. That baby clothes I bought at Sears were better made and lasted longer than those I got at Target. That when I was buying baby things, I was apparently invisible to store clerks.

Once at JC Penney, I tried to buy underwear for Anne. I stood near the cash register, purchase in hand. The store clerk looked me in the face and then served the women customers to my left and right. After she ignored me several more times, I waved the bag above my head to get her attention and finally succeeded. It was as if I wasn't supposed to be there, so I didn't exist for her.

Dr. Spock recommended establishing routines, patterns, and rituals, but not rigidly so. With input from Anne's two grandmas—Irene and my mom, Betty—I put schedules in place for feeding, bathing, play, and sleeping, but they were flexible. When we visited family and friends, I brought the portable crib, and later a portable playpen, for her safekeeping along with extra Pampers, clothes, favorite foods. Our car was packed when we traveled to meet family or friends. Sometimes I could hardly see out the side or back windows.

I learned that there were witching hours for both Anne and Billy. Regular bedtimes were needed and observed, 7:30 p.m. for Anne being the latest. If we were somewhere other than home, we folded up shop and left. Anne seemed comfortable when we followed these rules of the game, less so when we didn't—fussing, crying, and even coming down with colds when the schedule got too erratic.

She was an expressive baby, smiling and attentive to those who interacted with her. We were all drawn to her, especially her two grandmothers. Like Sue, Irene had eagerly awaited Anne's birth, writing to a close friend, "Dare I say it as an avowed humanist, but I have been praying all the time for this girl's arrival." With Sue's death, Anne was now the priority.

For my mom, Anne was special for more than one reason. My mom's first child, my older sister, had died a day after her birth. Mom's experience was awful: after a difficult delivery, her baby was taken from her without explanation. Twenty-four hours later, when my dad entered her room, she asked to hold her baby girl. My dad said, "Betts, I'm sorry. She didn't make it. They couldn't save her." Mom later had two boys—my brother, Jim, and me—but no other girls.

I'd read that the loss of a child is the most significant loss an adult can experience, beyond loss of a partner, health, money, status, or anything else. Anne was not a replacement for her grandmothers' lost daughters, but her presence, and her needs, touched deep feelings in both of them, and each treated her with consummate attention and affection. Anne and I were both lucky that they were in her life as a baby and would be for decades to come.

Not everyone had singular feelings of affection for baby Anne all the time. One afternoon, I heard her cry while she was in her crib. I went upstairs to her bedroom and picked her up. Billy was standing in the hallway corridor nearby.

"Billy, do you know why Anne was crying?"

"Well, I don't know for sure."

"Billy?"

"I might have come into her bedroom and maybe grabbed her toes a little bit."

"You mean you pinched her toes until she cried."

"Well sort of. You know I love my baby sister a lot, but I just don't like the idea of her being here."

"I know it's hard to have her here, but no more of that stuff. Okay?" And there wasn't, at least not that I knew of.

Besides the children's grandmothers, I tried to stay connected to our other family members, friends, and neighbors. I wanted my kids to feel that they were part of a larger community. I asked other folks to join us for activities and to do things with the kids when I didn't have time—things like making snow forts in the winter, reading them stories, playing board games. The kids' grandparents and I agreed on the expectations for behavior and what consequences made sense if Billy and later Anne misbehaved.

None of these things were different from what other caregivers would do, but that was the point: even though the kids had lost their mother, their needs could still be met. And I wanted them to have strong, healthy relationships with those who could take my place, in the event of my death.

Irene and I kept looking for a daytime nanny. An older woman made a two-hundred-mile bus trip from northern Minnesota to visit for a weekend. She came with presents for the kids, a booming voice, and supreme confidence: "What you need here is me. These little ones will find out what mothering is all about." While with us, she chain-smoked and ate little. One of her references was her son, who told me that she was a severe alcoholic and her most recent release from a state hospital had been two months earlier. When I asked her why she hadn't told me about her background before she came, she said, "Would you have hired me if I had told you the truth? I thought my son wouldn't say anything and I could try again."

In late June, we met Mimi. Early middle-aged, she was a delightful person, a recent arrival in the Twin Cities whose daughter had left home for college. She was looking for a short-term job while she put her life together. She was lively, energetic, warm, and good-humored. Her references checked out, and we needed help immediately, even if it wouldn't be permanent. The grandmothers—who were careful about their endorsements—liked her. We agreed that she would live at my house Sunday night through Thursday dinnertime. She cared for the children, made meals, and did light housekeeping. I found a cleaning service for heavy-duty work. My mom (Nana, to Billy and Anne) came on Fridays; Ad and Irene pinch-hit during the week, if needed, and sometimes took the kids for a Saturday or Sunday. We had hatched a plan.

Mimi proved to be all we had hoped for. She was responsible and caring, lighthearted but thoughtful. I asked Billy how he liked her. He had priorities: "I like her blond hair and that she laughs a lot." Mimi brought a light touch to a family that had been traumatized.

She and I related easily but carefully. We weren't that different in age and needed to agree on our parenting responsibilities while sharing the same space. I offered her my bedroom, which was on the same floor as the bedrooms of the children. I moved to the basement level of the house, which was not in the best shape—water sometimes slipped in from heavy rains—but it was livable. I had a large cardboard clothes closet, a desk with a lamp, and a full-size bed. A bathroom was down the hallway past the laundry room. The basement didn't have insulated walls, but with a space heater, it was warm enough. It was also two floors away from Anne's nightly feedings, which Mimi volunteered to take care of. I was no longer so exhausted.

When I moved to the basement, I put Sue's beautiful beige and gold wedding dress, a few other clothes, her jewelry box and jewelry, and pictures of her from our bedroom into our attic. I thought that, at some time, Anne might be interested in these things. With Mimi now in our bedroom, I couldn't keep Sue's things there, and I didn't want to make any room in the house a kind of shrine to Sue by keeping everything of hers in one place. We did have pictures of her in other rooms and volumes of photo albums.

As I took her things out of our bedroom, I felt as if I were moving in slow motion. A pale blue dress in one arm, a lovely white blouse with a starched collar in the other, shoes that would never be worn again—all were part of who she was, of how she had lived life. Letting go of them felt like letting go of her.

In these early months after her death, I missed her. Moving her clothes was wrenching. The letters she was writing or reading no longer sat on the end table near our bed. Unless Billy asked to join me, I slept alone. I missed my favorite foods she made—chicken curry, chili, cherry pie. Whenever I saw someone in large sunglasses or a colorful headband, I thought of Sue.

Sometimes I caught myself talking to her. Once as I was heading toward a hallway closet where we stored toilet paper, I said, "Honey, did you put toilet paper in the closet?" Another time I walked into the kitchen and asked, "Did you put coffee on?" Billy, who was seated at our kitchen table, gave me a confused look. "Dad, you okay?" he asked.

At night, I frequently paged through our many photo albums, where her pictures—our pictures—caught her look, her personality, her activities, the person who had been in our lives. Once, after looking at photos, I walked into our dining room and began circling our table, as I had done the afternoon she died. I remembered holding Anne in my arm, hearing the questions of the police officer, seeing the paramedics carrying the green bag in which they had put Sue's body. I had my eyes closed, but I saw everything that had happened. Tears came.

When Sue died, I was a graduate student. I had one summer class left and then comprehensive exams to take and my dissertation to write. With Mimi aboard, I thought I could work full-time and keep progressing toward my PhD. I finished the last course and studied for the exams, scheduled for August 6, which would have been our seventh wedding anniversary. I spent that day in a quiet classroom at the university, writing in longhand, filling many blue books with my responses. A few days later, my advisor called, congratulating me on having passed.

His call came in the morning before I stepped into the shower. As the warm water poured over my head, I felt alone. I realized that had Sue been alive, we would have celebrated. Her stepfather and her stepbrother had earned PhDs. She knew what it took each step of the way, and she had always been supportive of my efforts. The big moment had come and gone. I took pride in it, but it was very clear to me that the next steps would be harder still without her or the friendship and help of a new partner or love, which seemed unlikely.

CHAPTER 6

The First Summer After

⸜ ⸜ ⸜

With Mimi settled in, Ad, Irene, Billy, Anne, and I prepared to go up north, as huge numbers of Minnesotans do each summer. We would be visiting Ad and Irene's cabin near Bemidji, a college town in northern Minnesota about a four-hour drive from Minneapolis. I thought that taking baby Anne, who was five months old, could be a challenge, but was counting on Ad and Irene to help me make it work.

The cabin was on Mekenok Island, which we reached in a five-minute motorboat ride from the landing area. It was heavily forested, and many of its cabins were hidden from view from the shoreline and from our boat. The island often seemed mysterious, an undiscovered place.

Going across the lake to the island was typically a quiet experience. Loons would dive underwater as we approached them without emitting their loud calls. A few folks who were fishing would nod at us without speaking. It was rare to see speedboats or water-skiers or tubers. If the winds picked up, the waves pushed hard against our motorboat, one of the few sounds we heard. On many trips, we wouldn't talk much with each other. We were thinking about the day ahead.

Our family owned one of the eight log cabins on the island. Built in 1911, it was rustic at best, with no insulation, electricity, bathroom, television, radio, record player, or clocks. Its water system was unpredictable. There were insects, sometimes bats, ticks in the woods, and leeches near the shoreline. But we loved our cabin life and had vacationed there many times when Sue was alive.

On this visit, we shared the cabin with Ad's son Bart; his wife, Cindy; their daughters, Val and Cary; and their son, Brett, who was seven months older than Billy. We canoed, sailed, fished, swam, played on plastic air mattresses in the water, and sunned on the dock.

The kids loved swinging on the truck tire hanging from a long rope on a huge elm tree, flying nearly twenty feet above the ground. They invited the other kids on the island to join them in drawing and coloring, playing board and card games, and kicking soccer balls outside.

At night, each of the younger kids, favorite stuffed animals in hand, crawled under mosquito netting into the bed, futon, rollaway, or sleeping bag of their choice—some by themselves, some with Bart, Cindy, or me. Using flashlights, we read them stories until they fell asleep.

When we adults weren't with the kids, we made wonderful meals, visited with neighbors, and talked and talked and talked among ourselves inside, outside on the grassy hills, or on the dock.

Each day, the sun shone brightly on the lake water, breezes moved the cattails and tall reeds, duck families swam near our dock, and the calls of loons sounded during the day and especially at twilight. We were lucky to have no heavy winds or thunderstorms. At night, in the clear northern Minnesota sky, the moon and stars were especially visible. Mekenok was wild and unpredictable and beautiful. It was a refuge from the demands of work and city life.

One morning, I took Billy and Brett fishing in our motorboat. We had many nibbles—to the boys' delight—but no catches, though we came close. Both boys had their lines in the water when Billy's was pulled down.

"Dad, I've got something. It's heavy," he said. He could hardly hold up his pole. He slowly reeled in the line while I grabbed the pole, trying to keep it up.

When the fish got closer to the boat, just under the water, we all saw it. It was a huge northern pike. I reached for the fishnet to capture it, but as I did, it jumped out of the water, twisted in the air, and snapped the line. Billy fell over backwards, stunned. "It got away," he said. "Ohhhh." It was a shock for all of us.

Before I could say anything, Brett said, "Billy, you did great. You almost got him. I wish you had, but, boy, that was something."

Brett had said the right thing. We'd go out again.

On the Fourth of July, we had a potluck supper with our neighbors and watched the fireworks from a nearby grassy hill, some of us wrapped in blankets and warm sweaters. Many of the older children waved sparklers, and some young people lit bottle rockets that flew up and then exploded above us in surprising patterns of color that illuminated the island. Different homes, different religions, different politics, different ages, different jobs—nothing mattered. In its wildness and beauty and joy, Mekenok brought us together as a community.

At dusk on our last day, I sat by myself on the dock, looking past the reeds that shifted in the wind in front of me, toward the white gold of the sun's rays on the lake water. As twilight approached, the sun, orange and then red, slipped behind the line of trees on the distant shoreline—a sight Sue and I had shared many times. It was calm and beautiful. I missed Sue, but I still loved life on the island. The week at Mekenok had renewed my hopes for our futures: Billy's, Anne's, and mine.

In early August, Billy and I joined Bob at his family's cottage in Ocean Park, Maine. The cottage, which was near the beach, was a two-story wood-frame building with wraparound porches on both levels and a witch's tower above the second floor. Brown with yellow trim, it had an annex—a smaller two-story building attached to it. Bob's mother had had it built as a summer home for her and her eight children following the death of her husband. Sue visited nearly every summer from childhood through her college years. She had introduced me to it on our honeymoon.

Most of its dark walnut furniture predated World War II, as did all the dishes, glasses, utensils, cookware, and candlesticks in the house. Blue-and-white checkered curtains hung in the dining room; brass lights and framed photo collages decorated the walls. Relatives, many long passed, smiled in black-and-white and color photos, typically in beach scenes. There was a stone fireplace and no phone.

To reach the cottage, we followed Ocean Park Boulevard for two miles under the bower made from tall red pine trees located on either side of the road, past the Baptist assembly hall, the community library, the tennis courts (which on Sundays didn't open until noon), and the ice cream parlor. There were a few small restaurants and a post office. I loved the cottage and Ocean Park. Both were without pretense or modernity; for me, they were always restful and calming places.

In the late afternoon on the first day of our stay, Bob, Billy, and I walked on the beach. The tide was out. Seagulls flew just above our heads. People sunned in chairs and on blankets or slept under red, blue, and white umbrellas. Teenage boys tossed a football back and forth. A huge brown wooden pier stretched into the ocean. The breeze pushed the tall green grass against narrow wood-and-wire fences built to prevent erosion. As it grew cooler, we headed to the boardwalk and back to our cottage. We said little to each other, lost in the feel of the beach.

On Sunday, family members gathered with us at the beach for a potluck supper and storytelling. The aunties and young cousins recounted times with Sue and Bob—often wistfully, it seemed, but joyously, too. Sue had readily attracted attention with her tanned good looks, colorful clothes, and stories of Hawaii. She had been popular with other children and eventually boys, comfortable with others and in herself, adept at building friendships with strangers and sustaining relationships with family. Many recounted playing golf or tennis or going bodysurfing with Bob, whose spontaneity and friendliness they appreciated.

The family welcomed me, despite suspicions about my political views and my palpable ignorance about New England. Once I excitedly commented to Aunt Elizabeth about the beach being larger at different times of the day.

"It's the tide, Tim," she said, smiling. "Something you don't have in Minnesota?" I got the message that as a Midwesterner, I had a few things to learn.

After the family had gone, Bob told me of a recurring dream he had been having since Sue's death.

"I was in my bathing suit on the beach facing the ocean. Sue walked up to me and joined me. I got up to greet her and said, 'I'm so happy you came back. This is the happiest moment of my life. I'd heard even that you were dead, and now I know you didn't really die.'

"'Yes, Daddy. Let me tell you something about that.'

"Then I'd wake up and find myself crying. It's hard to accept that she's gone. Not a whole lot easier now than in April."

The next day was sunny and warm, with a light ocean breeze. Bob, Billy, and I drove to the small nearby airport in Biddeford. In the car, I held the urn that contained Sue's ashes. When we arrived, we discovered that the rental plane, a red and white Cessna, was a two-seater. Used chiefly for skywriting and banner towing, it was only big enough for the pilot and one passenger. We decided that I should go.

The plane flew along the beachfront, close enough for me to see people swimming and bodysurfing. I intended to drop Sue's ashes by our family cottage, which was close to the beach. When I saw it, I took the lid off the urn and slid the window open on my side. But, unexpectedly, I started to cry. I found I couldn't lift the urn to the window. We flew on.

The pilot asked, "Is there another spot?"

"No, please go back to where we saw the brown and yellow cottage."

When we approached a second time, I put my arm out the window and shook the urn. Sue's ashes scattered along a jagged line in the air. I could see them floating, hundreds of tiny specks, flying apart, dropping toward the area where the waves met the sand. As I shook the urn, I said, "Goodbye, sweetie. Thank you for Billy and Anne. I love you." As the plane shifted away from the beach, the wind hit my face, drying the tears that were edging down my cheeks and nose.

When we landed, Billy said, "We saw you go up. I was kind of worried that you might crash, but Grandpa said everything was okay. Can we go to McDonald's now?" I looked at Bob, who managed a weak smile. A cup of coffee for the grownups seemed about right.

CHAPTER 7

More Nannies

✳ ✳ ✳

When we returned to Minneapolis, Irene greeted me with the news that Mimi had quit. She had a chance to work as a legal secretary in a law office, where pay and benefits far exceeded what I could afford. Although I was sorry that she was leaving, I was grateful for her help throughout our crisis, which had given us, however briefly, a sense of optimism and hope about the future. When I told Billy that she would be going, he said, "I've had two good mommies so far. Maybe I'll get another."

We reactivated the search process for a live-in nanny, with Irene again vetting the candidates and me interviewing them. Between working full-time and single parenting, I had no time to give to my doctoral program, specifically to planning my dissertation research. I decided that I would go back to it when I could.

Four and a half months had passed since Billy lost his mother. At age five, he was headed to kindergarten in a new school. In these months, he turned in on himself. He was more quiet, less spontaneous and exuberant. He often played by himself, with Lincoln Logs, cowboy figures, Legos, toy cars. He collected comic books and football cards. He drew pictures frequently and with skill. One sketch was of himself, with bright eyes, a sly smile, and a cavalier look. He drew Columbus's ships—the *Niña*, the *Pinta*, and the *Santa María*. Sailors were flying off the ships in heavy storms. "They'll come back," he said. "It's just a rough trip."

He grew more curious about and attentive to his little sister: "Is she just going to eat that soft stuff?" "How long before she crawls?" "When is she going to talk?"

Sometimes when I read him stories from the Richard Scarry books we had, I'd sit Anne in my lap with Billy at my side. He'd put his hand lightly over her little legs. I loved his gentleness and the feeling of both children sitting near me—a benefit of being their dad. Family and friends noticed how quiet and patient Billy was, and the fact that he didn't act out with anger or show signs of depression. However, as one person said, "He's pulled in his wings a bit." And he rarely talked about Sue.

With me, at home or elsewhere, he continued to be his old curious, mischievous self. He was a well-behaved, cooperative child. I worried about how his mom's death was affecting him and also about his safety.

More than once, I had a dream in which he was crossing the street by himself when a car came speeding at him. I was standing on our front steps, yelling at him to run, but his back was turned, and he didn't hear me. I ran into the street and hurled myself, my body horizontal, trying to push him away, when the car hit both of us. He flew in the air, and I awoke, panting. The dream was always terrifying. Sue's sudden, unpredictable death hung over both of us.

Before long, Maria entered our lives. A dark-haired, large, strong woman, she came to the nanny interview with two loaves of bread she had made—"one for each kid," she said. She had grown up in Cuba, married a US Navy man from rural Minnesota, and lived with him on his farm for ten years before they divorced. She had childcare experience and lived in an apartment only a few miles away. Her references checked out.

"I can do anything—cook, clean, shop, take care of the little ones, do your yard," she said with confidence. "You name it and I can do it. You see, Maria will make you a home." We believed her. She moved in with us on October 1.

During that first month, Maria was as good as her word. She paid attention to both children. She listened to Billy and talked with him about his cars, toy soldiers, cards, books, friends, anything. She handled housekeeping jobs well and was a versatile cook, providing interesting rice dishes and lots of Midwestern favorites like fresh bread and apple pies.

Almost any time I came home from work, she would be in the kitchen, holding Anne in one arm and mixing something with the other hand, Billy supervising intently. She was a hugger, too—a physical person, comfortable with touch, a good thing for two little children who had lost their mom.

Fall began changing to winter. While the seasons changed, our lives seemed to be stabilizing. One night when I had finished reading a story to Billy, he said, "Maria, she's going to be okay. She's kind of noisy when she gets on the phone during the day—she talks really loud and fast—but I like her. So do Andy and Zac. We had the bread today that she makes. It's really good, Dad—you should try it." I did. He was right.

As Mimi had, Maria stayed with us Sunday night through the Thursday dinner hour. On Fridays, I brought my mother from her home in St. Paul for the day and sometimes for the night, too. With support in place, I had a little more free time for a social life. I'd go to a movie by myself or, on occasion, on a blind date with someone new. Oddly, though, when I wrote down a phone number or address for a woman on note paper that I had left by my nightstand or by the phone in the kitchen, the notes seemed to get misplaced or disappear. *How could I be so forgetful?* I wondered.

One weekday night, after the children were asleep, I decided to go to a movie by myself at a nearby theater. I put on my jacket and stopped in the living room to tell Maria that I was going out. She said coldly, "You going out tonight with a woman? Again?" I was surprised, both by the question and by her tone.

"I am going out to a movie, Maria, and that's really my business."

"You think so maybe." As I backed the car down the driveway, I felt uncomfortable but decided to let it pass.

The next night she apologized for her remarks, and we began a long conversation about her past. She had grown up on a farm in Cuba and met her American husband at Guantánamo Bay. They were both teenagers then. She returned with him to Royalton, a small town in central Minnesota, where they farmed. They married and had three children, but they fought about everything. "When he drank, we fought even more," she said. At times she was so furious with him that she hit him, once with a rolling pin. He hit her back. In their small community, people learned about their problems.

A social worker from the county interviewed both of them and recommended to the courts that their children be placed in foster homes, having concluded that neither of them was a fit parent. Maria told me, "That social worker, what she did was bad. If I had seen her again, I would have hit her, too." She and her husband had one more fight—"Very bad, Mr. Delmont"—during which she grabbed a sharp carving knife but didn't use it on him.

After their divorce, the courts declined to award custody of the children to either her or her husband. She had left Royalton ten years ago and hadn't seen her husband since then. She sometimes saw her children, "but not that often. This is why I like taking care of children now," she said. I thanked her for telling me her story, and we said good night to each other.

I found the casual way she described her violent behavior to be chilling—she showed lots of energy but no remorse. I was uneasy with this new information, none of which had been available to us when we had done our reference checks on her. I wondered whether Billy and Anne might be at any risk, for whatever reasons, in her company, but hadn't seen a reason to be concerned and so didn't do anything immediately.

The next night, I had to attend a dinner meeting. I told Maria of my plans and went upstairs to change clothes. When I came back down, she was furious: "So you are going out again, heh!" She opened and then slammed several of the kitchen cabinet doors, turned away from me, and shouted, "So go!"

That night I had a dream that Maria charged into my bedroom with a carving knife raised above her shoulder, heading for me—like in the famous scene from the movie *Psycho* in which Tony Perkins, in a granny dress and wig, stabs Janet Leigh through the shower curtain. I woke up, my heart beating fast; I was hyperventilating. I had an early breakfast meeting in the morning, so I didn't see Maria.

When I came home that night, I found a note from her on my bed: "Dear Mr. Delmont, I can make you a very good wife. I will take care of the little ones and be a cook. You should not bother with these younger women. They are not as good as me. Love, Maria."

After I read this, I sat on the bed with it in my hands for a moment and then went downstairs. I told Maria I would have to talk with her after the kids went to bed. She nodded.

Later that night I said, "Maria, I am not attracted to you, and I do not want to marry you."

She exploded. "You are lucky someone as good as me came into this house to do this work! I can do a lot better than this! I can get a lot better man than you."

"If that is the way you feel, Maria, I want you to go."

"I will go right now."

"Stay tonight—it's late. You can go tomorrow."

"I'm not staying here."

She went to her bedroom and started packing. I heard her talking to herself, but I couldn't make out the words. I went into the upstairs hallway to see what I might do. She breezed past me and went up into the attic to get her suitcases. "I called a taxi. I don't need you."

She continued to clear her clothes out of her bedroom closet, carrying dresses past me along with her suitcases. For a while I stood in the hallway, watching her. I decided there wasn't really anything I could do except get ready for bed.

After I heard her leave, I looked into her bedroom. Except for the furniture, it was empty. The front door and storm door were wide open; they swayed in the night breeze. Up the block, I could see the red taillights of the taxi, whiffs of exhaust rising from its tailpipe. I sighed, partly out of relief that she was gone, but partly because the nanny search would have to start yet again. After Sue's death, we had had two and a half months of freelancing, then Mimi for two months, then Maria for one month. We were headed in the wrong direction.

A few weeks before Christmas, Maria appeared at our front door. She was dressed beautifully, in a brown fur coat, collar, and hat. She carried an enormous number of wrapped presents in both arms and was smiling broadly.

"These, these are for Billy and Anne and for you, too."

I thanked her but said we couldn't accept them.

"Okay." Her smile faded a bit. "I will take them back." She turned around and headed to the taxi that had been waiting for her. We never saw her again.

During the Christmas season, Billy, Anne, and I spent much of our time with Irene and Ad and had a long visit with my mom. We watched *Sesame Street*, went to a *Nutcracker* ballet performance, and shared presents with family and friends. Ad read to Billy the life story of Fran Tarkenton, the Vikings quarterback (who, a month later, would lead his team to the Super Bowl). Billy had given Ad the book, the first Christmas present he had bought with his savings. Wearing his favorite purple jersey, the #44 of Vikings running back Chuck Foreman, Billy listened with full attention, snuggled next to his grandpa.

The highlight of Christmas for me was Ad and Billy's annual Christmas Eve nighttime walk, hand in hand, snowflakes falling on their shoulders and lit by a bright full moon. As I watched them through the window, I was grateful for the loving care my little boy was getting. That year we followed all the traditions we usually experienced when Sue was with us but spoke little about her absence. We were not in denial—just, as some might say, soldiering on.

Our third live-in nanny, Carolyn, was a former elementary school teacher and a single parent whose son, Tim, was two years older than Billy. While she and Tim stayed with us for five months, we saw her less than we had seen either Mimi or Maria. She was ill much of the time, stayed in her room at night, and was a very quiet person.

Despite the challenges, she was a responsible nanny and treated both Billy and Anne with kindness. Tim and Billy got along well and shared their toys, blocks, and games, although Tim spent a lot of time with his mother in their rooms. It was a kind of strange interlude, almost as if there were friendly ghosts in the house, but our home environment was stable, and that's what mattered to me.

Carolyn and Tim lived with us during one of Minnesota's characteristic long winters, which lasted from November to April. Snow accumulated over fifty inches, aided by a few blizzards, about average for Minnesota. In December and January, temperatures often fell below zero, so being outside for only a few minutes could lead to frostbite. Experiencing that kind of cold, which occurred occasionally, was irritating, frustrating, even scary. I took precautions for the kids: stocking caps, heavy scarves, warm mittens or gloves, snow pants and boots, and extra layers of clothing. Every parent I knew had a checklist. We were lucky that neither Billy nor Anne got bad colds or worse that year, something most kids experienced.

Winter had its joys, too. I took the kids sledding at parks and golf courses, and we built snow forts, had snowball fights, and even went skiing occasionally. Sometimes we walked outside as the snow was falling or after a storm ended to see the snow-covered tree branches, bushes, hills, and walking paths.

After each snowfall, I shoveled our driveway, steps, and sidewalk. Occasionally, when the snow was over four or five inches, I used our snowblower. There were nights when I was shoveling, after I had put Billy and Anne to bed, and stopped to take in the wintry scene. The sky would be dark blue, the moon a bright white, partially hidden by smoke that billowed from the chimneys of other houses on the block. I could see my breath hanging in the air. To me, Minneapolis in winter wasn't the frozen, inhospitable place that some people said it was.

In February we'd cross the river to go to St. Paul for the winter carnival. There would often be a huge castle built of ice blocks near the frozen Mississippi River in downtown St. Paul. We'd go view the ice sculptures glistening under streetlights in a downtown park or stand outside or in a packed auditorium to watch a parade.

That winter, I began writing notes about the activities I shared with the kids, conversations I had with Billy and family members, feelings I was experiencing as a single father. I wanted to share my memories with the people I loved. I thought that when Billy and Anne were older, they might want to know about how we had lived our lives after Sue had died. I wanted to remember what it had been like for me, too. I jotted notes on the backs of envelopes and slips of paper, whatever was handy. I would do this for many years to come, documenting our story.

I also kept up our photo albums, for which Sue had been previously responsible. She and I both valued them. Across decades, we kept taking photos that went into new albums. When the children were much older, I asked them, "If our house burned down, what is one thing you would want to save?" Both said, "The photo albums for sure, Dad."

In late spring, Carolyn and Tim left. Carolyn had found a full-time job in a county government agency, with good pay and benefits, and was ready to move on. Billy appeared to take her and her son's departure in stride. He was looking forward to the summer, when he said he'd have more time to spend with Andy and Zac, his neighborhood buddies.

Good luck rather than a careful search brought us our next nanny. One evening, a local babysitting service sent a friendly older woman to our home. Her name was Eldora. She was slightly built, with flowing red hair and a ready smile. Following her husband's death, she had begun doing temporary babysitting. She was a hit with Billy and very comfortable with Anne. I asked whether she might consider working for us on a trial run. She came, liked the work, and liked us. We agreed that she would be with us Monday through Thursday, 8:00 to 5:00. Mom agreed to continue coming on Fridays.

In June, Eldora began a relationship with us that would last for five years, never missing a day. I didn't know then that over this period she would contribute immensely to the stability and well-being of our home life. Mostly I was relieved that I had found her, could afford to pay her salary, and felt I could trust her with my children.

CHAPTER 8

A Welcome Romance

※ ※ ※

During that long winter, Billy and I visited Ad and Irene in Honolulu, where they had retired. By paying part of our travel expenses, they made our trip possible. We had a wonderful experience in warm, sunny weather—we saw the USS *Arizona* Memorial, participated in a luau, and spent a lot of time at the beach.

A few days before Billy and I returned home, some friends from Minneapolis who'd moved to Hawaii invited the four of us to dinner. They also invited Liz, a single parent, a close childhood friend of Sue's, and a friend of Irene's for over twenty years. I thought she was stunning—tall, tanned, slim, very pretty, with brown eyes and long brown hair, a ready smile, and a kind, warm manner.

Throughout the evening, Liz and I talked about Sue, about being single parents—each of us with two small children—and a bit about our jobs, with modest attention to the others. Two nights later, she hosted a dinner for us and for her family members, including her daughter, Lilly, and son, Keith. I was excited to see her again.

After Ad, Irene, Billy, and I returned to their condo, I borrowed my in-laws' car to go back to be with her. I stayed the night and returned about 6:00 a.m., which allowed barely enough time to pack for our flight home that morning. I was dazzled by Liz and by the incredible good luck that a blind date engineered in Hawaii had worked.

Liz and I immediately wrote each other letters and continued an almost weekly exchange for months. We shared open, giddy, romantic feelings.

We got to know each other through our letters. We talked about our kids and how we parented them, the kinds of relationships we had with our families, the work we did (she was a high school art teacher), and what we valued in relationships in and outside of the workplace. Counseling had helped her cope with a divorce from her children's father, who remained in their lives, as it had in my relationship and marriage to Sue.

Her letters showed me her warmth, caring, openness, comfort with feelings, ease of connection to me, many of the personal qualities required for a long-term relationship.

Sending and receiving letters was a gift, especially when long-distance telephone calls were very expensive. I read every letter from her as soon as it arrived and reread them carefully after I had put the children to bed. Seeing her name and address on the envelopes was enough to make me smile, to make my day better. I was falling in love.

During late spring, we decided to see each other in Minneapolis in the summer, when we both had more flexible work schedules. We were on the front end of the relationship and hadn't discussed the practical issues of what to do if it edged us toward marriage. But she was coming five thousand miles to visit us. "Can't wait to see you and be close to you," she wrote.

Liz's twelve-day visit went wonderfully: family dinners, visits to our city lakes and amusement parks, downtime with the children, and quiet moments together deepened our relationship. We agreed that Billy and I would return to Honolulu later in June so that she and I and our children could spend time together before her kids headed to their father's for the rest of the summer.

Before Liz left, she and I and Billy went to see *Star Wars*. In the theater, Billy sat between the two of us. Several times during the movie, I looked at both of them and smiled. I couldn't help myself. It felt so natural, so right to be together. Billy was excited by the story, its fantastic special effects, energy, imagination—everything. The movie had just been released in May, and its toys were in stores now. "When can I get some figures, Dad?" he asked. "And ships, too? I've got money."

"This weekend," I said.

Billy quickly built a full collection of miniature figures, including all the heavyweights: Luke Skywalker, Han Solo, Princess Leia, Chewbacca,

R2D2, and Darth Vader. He played endlessly with them. One night I joined him in his bedroom as he was playing.

I am not sure why, but I thought of the time when I was seventeen, a senior in high school. I had decided to give my collection of childhood toys to the children at the St. Joseph's Orphanage in St. Paul. It included my set of medieval knights, silver metal figures, some standing and some on horseback. They were my favorites, but I thought the kids could use them more than me. I described my collection to Billy and told him I was sorry that I hadn't saved them for him. He looked at me and said, "It's okay, Dad. I'm good. And you can play with me anytime you want."

After Liz returned to Honolulu, she sent me a card with a picture of two birds side by side, each with a red heart, their heads resting together. Inside she wrote, "My mind is still running over and around all the lovely experiences I was able to share with you. I'm so glad you're coming Wednesday! Thank you again for the super treatment . . . I feel like a queen. I LOVE YOU."

I wrote Bob that Liz and I were getting serious and, despite the short time of our relationship, the possibility of marriage later was real. I thought we might be one of those couples who build a successful marriage on a short courtship.

In our first days back in Honolulu, Billy and I spent time with Liz and her children at the beach, in parks, and over shared meals and did artwork together. It hardly seemed as if our two families had never been together before. I also met briefly with some friends of Ad and Irene who were administrators at the University of Hawaii and made inquiries about possible job openings in my field, if moving to Hawaii became a serious option. They said they weren't sure about openings but told me to stay in touch.

Liz and I and the kids then flew to Maui to spend time with Liz's sister, their father, and many other members of her family. The first night, over dinner and other activities, we began the process of introducing ourselves to them as a couple.

The next day, leaving our children with her family, Liz and I drove to some of her favorite spots on the island. In the car, she dropped a bombshell: "I've been thinking about our relationship, and I'm feeling scared. Things are moving too fast for me."

She told me she was feeling pressured and unsure about our future, about getting married. Hawaii was her home, where she had her support system. Moving to Minnesota scared her.

"I don't understand. I thought we were close and could take time to think through what we should do," I said. "We brought our kids together to see what would happen. I thought we'd go from here. I don't know for sure what's in the future."

But Liz said she wasn't in love with me, although she had strong feelings for me. That would take time for that to happen, if it ever did. Stunned, I asked her what had changed. She couldn't tell me; she said she didn't understand it herself.

In the morning, Liz took Billy and me to the airport. I was still in shock. At the gate to our plane, she and I hugged, tears in our eyes. We said we'd write. I walked part of the way on the ramp, then turned around and smiled at her, just a little. I didn't sleep much during the long flight. I missed her. As the plane flew over the ocean, the sun reflected at times off its wings, almost blinding me.

The first day home, Billy and I slid his matchbox cars down our driveway hill. Some made it all the way to the street, while others tipped over long before that.

"How did you like our trip?" I asked him.

"It was really fun. I like Keith and Lilly and Liz, too. And the beaches. Are we going back? Will I see them again?

"I don't know. I can't say if Liz and I are going to see each other anymore. It kind of looks like we won't, but I'm not sure. We'll see."

Liz and I continued to write each other, and she sent me birthday presents. I still wanted to hold on to our relationship, to somehow rebuild it, but it was gone. One of her letters couldn't have been clearer:

> I miss you and Billy naturally. I do feel that I suddenly got scared that things were moving too fast and in a direction I wasn't at all sure of. I still feel that way. I did think I was falling in love, but then my feelings changed directions. I feel if you lived here we would date, but I wouldn't want to be responsible for your moving over here. It would've been so nice to get to know you gradually and over a long

period of time under more normal circumstances. I think
we did have some very wonderful and meaningful times
together. Thank you for all you did for me . . . both in
Minneapolis and here. You are a very wonderful person.

Liz didn't know what caused her feelings to change, but she was honest
with me. And she was kind in the way she told me. I'd been dumped, but
about as nicely as possible. All I could do was accept it.

A few years later, Irene told me that friends of her in Hawaii had
mentioned that Liz had remarried. Without knowing anything about her
husband or the circumstances of her marriage, I told myself that I should
be glad for her and for her children, but I couldn't find that feeling. I saw
her helping Billy with his artwork, her hand on his shoulder, suggesting
a color to use. And feeding Anne her cereal in a highchair, laughing as
oatmeal dropped from the spoon to her own wrist. I was sad that my
children wouldn't have her as a stepmother, one who was clearly a kind,
nurturing, responsive person—one who would have changed their lives
for the better.

I felt sad for the breakup of our relationship, too. Some nights I lay
awake wondering how we might have done as a couple if we'd lived in
the same city. She and I had overcome many obstacles in building a relationship, but the distance was one of the largest. If we had sustained our
relationship, I wasn't sure what we would have done, but, with her change
of heart, we never really addressed other potential problems. Losing Liz,
after Sue's death, was hard to accept. I wasn't optimistic about future possibilities. How many times could I fall in love? How many women would
I even want to marry or would want to marry me? And could I find one
who'd make a good stepmother?

Many, many years later, long after my relationship with Liz ended, I
came to a different conclusion. I saw our romance, if not the breakup, as
a reason for hope—about my chances for a new love relationship, about
life itself. Two young people, single parents both, who lived five thousand
miles apart, considered and then began building a relationship. It was
unusual, it was unpredictable, it was full of obvious risks of failure—many
adults might not have begun it—but we had made progress. Under different circumstances, it might have worked.

CHAPTER 9

What Makes a Good Dad?

✳ ✳ ✳

That summer, I began to reflect on my role as my children's only parent. It had been fifteen months since Sue died. I thought that no one could replicate the caring and skills she could have brought to parenting Billy and Anne. That was a terrible fact, no matter how many of us stepped up to the challenge. Because of her death, I needed to broaden and deepen my role as a father—become even more purposeful and intentional. But I didn't have a good feel for what I should be doing for the kids as they got older.

I had some models for single parenting. I had lived with or heard about family members who were single parents, some of whose behaviors I could try to emulate. Following her divorce from my dad, my mom was a single parent for the rest of her life—another fifty-three years. When I was a teenager, every day she spent an hour or more each way riding the bus to and from her job. Before she left at 6:00 a.m., while I slept, she made me breakfast.

Her father, Grandpa Peter, had been a single parent for her and her seven siblings when his wife—my grandmother Elizabeth—was periodically confined to a state mental institution with a diagnosis of schizophrenia. Somehow, on Saturday nights, Grandpa Peter gave all the children baths and prepared their clothes for Sunday-morning church services.

Sue's mother, Irene, was a single parent for most of thirteen years following the divorce from and death of her first two husbands, respectively. In Honolulu, she taught additional college courses to make money for Sue's swimming and diving classes.

As single mothers and fathers, these relatives had been responsible and resilient, while sometimes making mistakes, as all parents do. I began to see them as guides who shared a universal message: "It's not about you. It's about your children." In my mind, I knew that, but my own first year of single parenting had driven the message in. I began to *feel* it, to understand it on a deeper level.

It meant that my priorities, especially those related to advancing quickly in my career, had to change. It meant that working long hours at my office or at home could not be a norm for me, although it was for most other university employees. It meant that doing the everyday things to keep a family going were valuable in themselves and worthy of doing well. The children had to come first, as they had in many ways for my mother and our family members. I didn't know why, but it took me a whole year to get it.

I began to question some of my long-held assumptions about what dads are supposed to do in family life. Before I married Sue, I thought that some roles were exclusively gender-defined—some are men's, some are women's—and that they had to be that way. The most important role for a man was to provide financial support for his family. I remember hearing from my mom when we talked about Grandpa Peter that he was a "good provider" and little else. That was how she saw him, and that was what she valued most about him.

Being a good provider meant showing up for the job each day and working hard and well. If necessary, it meant holding more than one job or working long hours or being called to work with little warning for an unknown period of time. My mom, my brother, Jim, and I lived with Grandpa Peter; each morning, Grandpa sat in our living room for ten or fifteen minutes before it was time for him to leave and catch his bus to his job. He made sure he was never late. For his generation, and those that followed, work outside of the home was a man's priority—the most significant source of his pride and identity. Management of the home life was a woman's.

Another prevailing notion when I became a dad was that men were to be the heads of their families: the parent with the most authority, the disciplinarian, the one who knew best and who was held in highest regard out of fear or respect by the children. With that status came almost no expectation that dads would equally share with their wives or partners all the roles of parenting and family life. Childcare and household chores, in particular, fell within a woman's purview.

That, again, had been my experience growing up. While my grandfather had been a single parent for part of his life, when we lived with him, he did no childcare or household work. Mom did the shopping, the cooking, the clothes washing, everything, even though she held a full-time job outside the house. I was grateful that Grandpa Peter had let my mom, my brother, and me stay with him, but during my childhood he was never meaningfully involved in my life—no stories read together, shared playtime activities, walks to the park, or attendance at my school events. Although we had family dinners, I can't remember a single conversation I had with him. He was not hostile, critical, or hurtful to me. He was invisible. I thought his behavior was the norm for grandfathers.

While I was growing up in St. Paul, the belief that men were the stronger, more accomplished gender was impossible to avoid. Among boys, "You play like a girl!" was not a compliment. When I became an adult and a dad, that notion was still prevalent. It referred to physical strength but much more; it meant that men did work for pay outside the home and controlled life within it because they were more thoughtful, more rational, not given to emotional reactions, and more stable and dependable. They were predisposed by their gender and cultural practice to lead. I became a parent at a time when these traditional ideas—these expectations—were still widespread throughout America, despite being challenged by leaders of the women's movement.

But after Sue's death, these notions about men no longer made sense to me. As a single parent, I needed to both work for pay and care for my children; they were equal priorities. Through my everyday involvement with Billy and Anne, I learned that being a rational, distant person with them was a misguided idea. They needed my touch, my communication, my caring reactions—all kinds of connections. I looked for and got help from many family members and friends, but I realized I had to change the traditional model of being a father that existed almost everywhere.

I got insights on being a single dad from a few studies. On one occasion, I had a conversation with Norman Garmezy, a professor of psychology at the University of Minnesota and a family friend. He told me about a thirteen-year study that he and his faculty colleagues had conducted on how resilience developed in youth who came from impoverished backgrounds in poor urban areas.

The study found that children who had at least one trusted adult present over a long period of time in their lives, one whom they felt loved and supported by, overcame their obstacles to become mature, responsible, happy people. The trusted adult could be anybody, not just a family member. I wanted to be that someone for Billy and Anne, so that they could emerge from childhood as resilient teenagers and adults. I felt encouraged by the findings of the study. If others had played that role effectively, why not me?

Shortly after my discussion with Professor Garmezy, a friend recommended a book, *Bachelor Fatherhood: How to Raise and Enjoy Your Children as a Single Parent*, by Michael McFadden. It was a book of anecdotes and opinions rather than a comparative research study, but its ideas jelled with the findings of Professor Garmezy's work. From his experience as a single father, McFadden concluded that children can prosper if they have at least one persistent attachment to an adult, whether a man or a woman.

He wrote that our society had begun to recognize the importance of single parenting in many ways, including the use of the term "single-parent family" instead of "broken home"—a respectful term replacing a shameful one. And he said that being a single father could be "transformational" for a man—it could open up new opportunities for growth and change.

The study and the book hit home for me. They added evidence to what I had seen in my family: that single parents, male and female, could function effectively; that even without partners they could create positive life experiences for their children. I took hope from that knowledge.

Most of the stories I read about single parenting documented that America's single parents were overwhelmingly women—depending on the source, an estimated 90 to 99 percent. As a single father, I was a rarity. I hardly thought about that. Mostly I saw myself as someone who had adult responsibilities in work and family life. Why wouldn't I feed my children? Or wash their clothes? Or ensure that they got needed medical care? Or keep them close to the family members who loved them?

One night after I had put Anne and Billy to bed, I walked past a bookcase in our second-floor hallway. I glanced at the covers of two books,

Childhood and Society by Erik Erikson and *Passages* by Gail Sheehy. Both addressed issues of human development and offered advice about how to move through life stages.

Sue and I had read and discussed both books. I took them off the shelf and paged through them. The findings jumped out at me. Erikson said that in the sixth stage of development, at twenty to thirty-nine years old, healthy people "learn what is important to them, successfully form loving relationships with other people, and raise their children . . . moving toward intimacy and away from isolation." Sheehy wrote that in the "Catch 30s" stage, people "deepen life commitments . . . begin sending out new shoots at 32, 33, or 34." I was thirty-three. Making a commitment to parenting my children as well as I could seemed absolutely consistent with where I was in life.

What was also clear was that I couldn't do everything by myself. I needed a family team and others outside the family for help. While in school or at work, I had been a member of many teams and projects, especially sports teams, student government organizations, and office work groups. Experiences on those teams helped me in forming a family team to raise Billy and Anne without Sue. The essentials were the same: find your roles, cooperate and support each other, communicate in a timely way, and stick to your goals and relationships. Our team consisted of two grannies, two grandpas, a daytime nanny, and me, with five of us living in the Minneapolis–St. Paul area in close contact with each other—so fortunate for me. With this team in place, I was never alone as a parent, although I lacked a partner. I learned how to work in a team that would sustain a joint child-raising effort for years. Like other men of my era who participated on teams, I was better prepared for single parenting roles and responsibilities than I initially realized.

Sue had had to overcome her own challenges to meet the needs of our children, and I owed it to her to follow her example. Very importantly, she had also encouraged me to take on nontraditional roles as her husband and the father of her children. She trusted me to do nightly feedings for Billy and Anne when they were babies, to care for them when they were sick, and to play with them almost any time. While we were married, I routinely did shopping, cooking, laundry, and some cleaning. From my experiences with other couples I knew, I learned that not all women—all mothers—fully welcomed these initiatives by their husbands. Sue was far more flexible than many.

I had been exposed to traditional concepts of fathering, but I was predisposed to and comfortable with accepting alternative values and putting them in play. Why was that? Yes, I had single-parent models in my family from which to learn, insights from research on the importance of being a mature, single dad, and support from Sue and others about my fathering activities, all to the good. But something ran deeper in me. On a very cold winter night in January—when the temperature fell to thirty degrees below zero and strong winds rattled our storm windows—I sat next to our fireplace, drawn by its warmth, to try to figure out why I was open to change, to understand the mystery.

I changed because I believed that I could take a risk and things would work out okay. That confidence had come, I thought, from the respectful and affirming way I had been treated as a boy, a teenager, and a young adult by my mom, by my brother, by an aunt who lived with us, and especially by many men. My dad was out of the picture, and I was not close to Grandpa Peter, but other men were there for me—something I hadn't anticipated.

There were many: The leader of my Boy Scout troop who, over three years, encouraged me to participate in all its summer and winter activities. The elementary teacher and coach who selected me as a starter on our baseball and basketball teams. My high school class advisor who wrote notes to my mother on how I was doing academically and socially. My B-squad basketball and varsity football coaches who gave me a chance to play and complimented me on my achievements. The advisor to our school newspaper who helped me believe I could be a success in college. The homeroom advisor who taught me how to drive a car *after* I had graduated, when no one else had offered. All these men helped me believe that I could grow up to be a fine person and a good man, someone with the potential to be a responsible father. I believed in myself because they had believed in me.

I had managed a crisis situation immediately after Sue's death and begun building a predictable family life for the kids and myself, despite the arrival and departure of three live-in nannies. Not small matters. I had the confidence to face future unknown situations. But I also realized I still had a lot to learn about parenting growing children.

CHAPTER 10

Friends and Neighbors

✳ ✳ ✳

In fall 1977, Billy started first grade at a new school one block from our house. He was old enough to walk back and forth by himself. He spent time with Andy and Zac, who lived close by. They rode bikes, played with their *Star Wars* toys, and drew pictures. They had sleepovers at each other's houses and went trick-or-treating together at Halloween. As I walked with them in the darkness through our neighborhood, past the carved pumpkins with their jagged, lighted smiles, I was grateful that he was a healthy little boy who found friends and happy experiences in safe surroundings.

In time, Billy warmed to Eldora. One day near Christmas, she smiled as she told me, "You know, Tim, today Billy let me hold his hand—for the first time." Gaining the confidence of small children requires patience, and Eldora had that and more. Each day at three o'clock when Billy returned from school, she made him his favorite snack: toast with cinnamon and brown sugar. Then, for a half hour, together they watched his favorite cartoon shows on TV while Anne usually napped. On some days, she took Billy and Anne shopping. Occasionally, she had sleepovers for the kids at her house. Week by week, Eldora and Billy grew closer.

With Anne, she was a hands-on nanny. They read stories, had tea parties, and went outside to play, even when it was cold. Eldora helped Anne learn words, numbers, colors, names, places—and manners. She also welcomed Beth, who lived across the street from us and, over time, became Anne's best friend. The three of them made cookies, played games, and watched television together. Disagreements between the girls didn't happen often, but Eldora—a mother of girls—knew how to handle them.

Mom cared for Billy and Anne on Fridays. An avid reader, she introduced the kids to a wide array of books, some of which she had read to me—the Hardy Boys series, *Goodnight Moon*, *Paddington at the Seashore*, *The Little Engine That Could*, *The Velveteen Rabbit*, *The Wind in the Willows*, and *The Tale of Peter Rabbit*. They walked with her to the local store for groceries and helped her make dinners. When they were older, she took them on the bus to downtown Minneapolis for sightseeing and lunch.

One Friday night, we agreed that Mom would stay with the kids while I went to see a movie after dinner. She planned to stay at our house overnight. When I put on my jacket and leaned down to hug and say good night to Anne, who was now about two years old, she wrapped her arms and legs around my leg. "Don't go, Daddy, don't go. Stay home," she said, tears running down her cheeks. I lifted my leg up trying to encourage her to let go, but she hung on with determination. Mom and I looked at each other and started to laugh—I couldn't get rid of the barnacle! We found our composure and together pried off little Anne, who was still crying. I kissed her and left her in Mom's comforting arms. It was one of many times that she extended her Friday stay to give me a break that I needed.

As Christmas drew near, I had a card made from a photo of Billy, Anne, and me sitting on a bench in Ad and Irene's backyard, holding hands, smiles on our faces. I sent copies to family and friends. Mom said the photo was too dark and everyone's hair was a mess, which was true, but I loved that picture—it seemed to capture our happiness, our closeness.

Billy helped me buy and wrap presents for mailing to Sue's stepbrother and his family, Grandpa Bob, and my brother, Jim, and sister-in-law, Sallie. They sent us presents, too. Staying connected at Christmas was important to us.

As in past years, we spent Christmas Eve and Christmas Day with Irene, Ad, and their friends. Irene gave Billy, Anne, and me matching pajamas, with red-and-white checkered tops and solid red bottoms—we would be recognizable wherever we went. At Christmas brunch, we each gave a toast and clinked our glasses together. In his toast, six-year-old Billy said, "This is for Mommy, that she is happy, too." His comment took our breath away, but we all clinked glasses with him. Later in the afternoon, we looked at photo albums of Sue and remembered Christmases past with her. We went to Mom's apartment in St. Paul for Christmas Day dinner and opened presents there. Christmas with the Minnesota grandparents was itself a gift, providing us continuity, especially in the early years after Sue's death.

I loved our neighborhood in southwest Minneapolis. We lived on Colfax Avenue, a heavily tree-lined residential street interrupted by a large public park, Lyndale Farmstead. The park's location lessened traffic, making our street safer for my kids. One-half block west of our house was a larger park, Lyndale Park, which surrounded Lake Harriet, one of Minneapolis's most popular lakes. Near the lake was the rose garden, a two-acre plot with two fountains and rows and rows of multicolored roses. Not surprisingly, the area was a draw, and many families with young children bought houses on our block.

Our house, built in 1911, was like others: two stories with an attic and a basement, a red brick foundation, a white stucco exterior, and black trim. Its first floor had a living room, dining room, and kitchen, with brown oak, beamed ceilings, a built-in buffet and bookshelves, a fireplace, and a sunroom. The second floor had four bedrooms and a bathroom. There was enough room for our immediate family, a nanny, and the many short-term visitors we hosted. The natural wood and lighting in the house gave it a warm presence, which we loved. It also needed few repairs or upgrades—a break for a family with little time or extra cash for making improvements. Although Sue had died in our second-floor bedroom, none of us ever felt uncomfortable in that room or other areas of the house. It was home, a place of comfort and refuge, not fear. I still live there.

I got to know our neighbors over the years. There were quarterly potluck suppers, many of which went late into the night. At one, a group of us stayed up all night and walked around Lake Harriet until 6:00 a.m. We had an annual summer block party, sometimes visited by Minneapolis police, who shared statistics on the number of crimes in our neighborhood and their perspectives on crime prevention. Community policing, in which police and citizens come to know each other, was in practice, if modestly. Some summer nights we'd sit on the hillside of a neighbor's front yard, wrapped in blankets, to watch movies projected on the side of a large moving van. A neighbor who worked for the county library system got them for us. The colors stood out in the darkness, even as we saw the clouds and stars overhead. On those nights, I felt especially safe.

We routinely looked out for each other's children when they played in the yards and on the street as well as for each other's property when someone was away from the neighborhood. These actions were more than backup for me—they were confirmation that we could build regard and trust among ourselves.

One winter morning, I found that extraordinary help was available, too. At 2:30 a.m., Billy woke up crying, saying his ear was hurting. I had heard his cry and thought that it was deeper than a typical wakeup cry. I held him and walked with him for a long time, but his pain and discomfort seemed to worsen—and he was a child who had a high tolerance for pain. I called one of my neighbors to ask if I could drop off Anne so that I could take Billy to the emergency room.

I put Anne in her winter clothes over her sleeper and Billy in his parka and, carrying both kids, headed to my neighbor's home. I walked slowly over the ice patches on the sidewalk as the wind blew snowflakes in my face. With a big smile, even though it was 4:00 a.m., Kay and Leigh answered their door and took Anne from me. I headed to the hospital and eventually got an antibiotic for Billy's ear infection. Kay cared for Anne and waited to go to work until Eldora arrived. That was just one of many times that my neighbors helped me out of a crisis.

As helpful as my neighbors were, however, there were situations from which neither they nor the Minneapolis police could protect us. On several occasions, thieves broke into our garage—once stealing Billy's bicycle while he and I were in our kitchen, the garage within view. I felt invaded; it was personal. Two other times, when the kids were older, there were sightings of a man who stopped his car on our street and in the nearby park area to solicit young girls. The possibility that Anne or other little girls could be molested horrified me. I walked with her anytime she was visiting friends until the sightings ended. I was fortunate to be raising my children in what was generally a safe and supportive neighborhood, but I still needed to be vigilant.

There were other threats over which my neighbors and I had little control. On one occasion Billy was watching television in our sunroom when he heard a loud sound outside the house like a freight train moving by. He turned his head and saw a huge elm tree from across the street falling toward our house. He yelled, "Dad, Dad! Help, we got to go!" as the top of the tree branches grazed the windows behind him. His shouts awoke me from a nap. I grabbed Anne's hand and ran downstairs, calling to Billy. We went quickly down to our basement. As we listened to city sirens, I turned on the radio to learn that a huge tornado had passed through Minneapolis, St. Paul, and many suburbs, devastating homes, businesses, playgrounds, parks, and bridges.

We left our basement and walked into a forest of downed trees. Some had collapsed the cars they fell on. Others blocked roads and sidewalks, making walking and even driving almost impossible. The air was still and the environment surprisingly quiet, even though large numbers of my neighbors were out inspecting the damages. We were stunned by what we saw.

I thought back to a storm from my childhood. An older man named Pinky Shriner was a custodian in my elementary school. He talked and laughed with us kids while he swept the floors in the building corridors or washed windows. We liked Pinky. One night during a rainstorm, strong winds broke a tree limb, which landed on the electrical wires leading to his house. The wires snapped, and sparks ignited a fire, which burned down most of the house. His wife, who was asleep inside, died in the fire.

My mom, Jim, and I went to a fundraiser to help with her funeral expenses. It was at Schmidt Brewery, a bottling plant near our home. Many outdoor dances were held there; this time was different. People drank beer from plastic cups and talked quietly with each other. There was no music and no sense of fun. A nice person, a wife and mother, had been killed by a horrible, unanticipated accident.

As I walked through our neighborhood with my kids, remembering that earlier storm and its tragic results, it occurred to me that if the tree that fell near our house had been five feet longer or five feet closer, it could have crashed through the windows, injuring or killing Billy. With my right hand, I took one of Anne's hands, and with my left, one of Billy's.

I held them tightly, aware of the unanticipated, of things from which—even with a partner—I could not protect them. I guided my kids out of the street, past the fallen trees, back to our home. I had seen enough for the day.

During this year, through a friend, I met Donna and her children, Johnny and Dannie, who were a few years older than Billy and Anne. Donna was a small, dark-haired woman with a ready smile. Separated from her husband, she was essentially a single parent. A nurse by training and a singer, she lived with multiple sclerosis, which had been diagnosed several years earlier, using canes and a wheelchair. She managed all her children's activities. Our families became close friends and shared meals, went on picnics, watched parades and sporting events together, and spent many Friday nights watching movies at one of our houses.

Since Donna and I did nearly all the cooking in our respective households, we routinely shared meal ideas and recipes. I had moved beyond tater-tot hotdish, mac and cheese, chicken wings, and burgers to beef and chicken shish kebabs, pork roasts, ham dishes, and Delmont spaghetti and lasagna, the latter drawn from a family recipe of my grandfather's.

Later, when Billy was in high school, he would develop an interest in cooking and help me make meals on the weekends. When he went to college, I gave him a collection of our family recipes, some of which I had shared earlier with Donna. She gave me her recipes for vegetable dishes and salads, which helped me grow my cooking knowledge and skills.

Donna exuded optimism, energy, empathy, and fun. She was a welcoming, caring, nurturing person. She had a self-deprecating sense of humor about most things with which she dealt, including her disability. She once said to me, "You know, I fall down getting out of bed every morning. Sometimes I land on my butt, sometimes on my side, but I can't get up by myself. It irks me, but I usually laugh sitting there on the floor. What else can I do?"

Our time together developed into an abiding friendship, rather than a romance. Equally importantly, Billy and Anne became friends with her kids. From Donna I learned how difficult it could be for a woman to be a single parent, especially with a disability, and how important it was for her—and how challenging it was—to build and sustain relationships with a wide circle of family and friends who could support her and her children. She worked very hard to be the best parent and person she could be while managing her physical challenges in everyday activities.

We talked about whether we parented our four kids—our boys and girls—similarly or differently. We couldn't identify much that separated us. We thought that kids needed structure in their daily lives—times for play, travel, education, eating, sleep, quiet—enough but not too much. They needed to be attended to, nurtured, and given emotional and physical support. They needed family and friends, people who were interested in them and with whom they could build relationships. They needed adults who were responsible and available, who held them accountable and upon whom they could depend.

Donna and I shared the same perspectives on parenting; our being different genders mattered little. We both thought that as the adults in the family, it was our job to take responsibility for managing the daily lives of our kids while doing the best we could to meet our own needs. We made the same kind of screw-ups as other single parents, too. Once she said, "Yesterday I fried one of Dannie's soccer shorts in the dryer. Shrunk it one size, maybe two. Poor kid, she didn't like that at all." Meanwhile I sometimes found it hard to schedule doctor appointments and remember to check that the kids had the right clothes for each change of season. I didn't always succeed in keeping both kids on a schedule. There were always things to do. Even with help from Eldora and the grandparents, single parenting was a twenty-four-hour-a-day reality.

Donna and I saw the movie *Kramer vs. Kramer*, in which a mother leaves her small child and her husband and then returns to claim the child as the custodial parent. It is a touching film, brilliantly acted by Meryl Streep and Dustin Hoffman. A central theme is whether women have innate attributes of mothering that make them more reliably effective parents than men, an assumption that guided custodial parenting decisions in most American family courts of that era.

The custodial parent had the child or children for six days a week or more, with the noncustodial parent seeing the child for no more than one day a week and for a defined period during summers, usually two to four weeks. With few exceptions, moms were the custodial parents and dads the noncustodial. This had been Bob's experience with Sue and my dad's with my brother and me. Coparenting or shared custody was not normalized.

Seeing the movie triggered many discussions between Donna and me about parenting attributes and styles and led us to the conclusion that maybe more mothers are better parents than fathers are—whether parenting together or singly—because they learn more about how to parent and their efforts are widely expected and supported in society. The prevailing thought of the time was that women were better parents than men because of inherent gender differences, but we weren't sure about that. We knew women whose parenting skills were limited. We thought, too—in a nod toward me—that men can learn to be very effective parents, a match to women, if opportunity arises and they want to.

Donna and I were friends while our children were young, but eventually our lives went in different directions and we lost touch.

CHAPTER II

Billy and Anne: Conversations

⌗ ⌗ ⌗

As Anne and Billy got older, I had extended conversations with them. I often didn't anticipate what we'd talk about or for how long. Their questions, their concerns, and their insights were all interesting to me.

Between ages two and three, Anne's confident, outgoing personality emerged—as did her independence. I was surprised and often delighted by what she did and said. I tried to listen carefully to her, to sense the feelings underlying her words; it was not my strongest skill but one I wanted to improve. Nearly every morning at 7:00 a.m., she trooped into my bedroom, gave me a big kiss and a hug, and made an announcement such as "It's morning. It's time to get up. You must get up now. I will help you out of bed. I want you to come. I am hungry now. Carry me."

We would watch snatches of television programs together, especially *Sesame Street*, *Mister Rogers' Neighborhood*, a few favorite cartoon shows, and, on several occasions, *Wonder Woman*. At the beginning of every episode, Wonder Woman would spin around, rays and sparks flowing from her, and her clothes would change into her superhero costume by the magic of 1970s TV special effects. Anne would watch this transformation intently but never commented on it.

One night I stood outside the bathroom door, watching her brushing her teeth. I wanted to see how she was doing on her own. She stood on a stool in front of the sink, unaware of me as she brushed. Then she jumped from the stool and landed in the middle of the bathroom floor. She raised both arms as high as they could go and began spinning round and round, her blond hair and white nightie flying. As she circled, she shouted, "I am Won-derr Woo-mannn!"

At the height of her spin, she suddenly stopped, her head tilting toward the doorway. She had figured out I was watching. She dropped her arms to her sides, pivoted around, and walked past me without speaking or acknowledging my presence. She went down the hallway to her bedroom. Shortly thereafter, I heard her voice: "Daddy, you may come and read me a story now." I smiled and thought, *Who's in control of this situation? Not me.*

Once, Eldora said, "Come on, little girl. We'll go outside to say good-bye to Daddy."

Anne replied, "I am not a little girl. I am a big girl. But I will go outside with you."

On another occasion, she was playing with a full-size broom and knocked it into the furniture and lamps. She tipped over one lamp and nearly broke it.

I said, "Put the broom back." She didn't. "Put the broom back." She smiled and still didn't. "Put the broom back or you will have to go upstairs to your room."

She paused, looked at me, and said, "I sweep now."

Like other children, Anne created imaginary friends. I loved seeing the look in her eyes and her smiles as she brought a new one to life or elaborated on their stories. And, of course, I played along. Alvin the Alligator popped out of paper bags to nip at Anne's nose or ears, which prompted lots of laughter from her. Ray the Workman fixed all kinds of toys, bicycles, cars, lawn mowers, pretty much anything that ran on wheels. Anne would say, "He has to go to school to learn about how to fix things, but I help him a really lot so he can go home and have his supper on time."

Most of all, we had conversations with Mr. Tree, who lived outside Anne's second-floor bedroom and had a personality suspiciously like that of Mr. Rogers. She would say, "Mr. Tree is kind. He listens to my stories. He keeps my secrets." She loved Mr. Tree and wanted him to stay close to our house as she grew up. That way they could always be friends.

In the summer when Anne was three, the real tree on the boulevard in front of our house—a very large, tall, beautiful elm—became infected by Dutch elm disease, which, if left unattended, would eventually kill the tree. Our neighbors and I inoculated our elm trees by injecting their roots with a pesticide to kill the beetles causing the disease. I did this for three years until the prevention was no longer effective and Minneapolis park board staff determined that the tree had to be cut down.

One afternoon, Anne and I looked out of a front bedroom window as the tree cutters began their work. Limbs disappeared quickly under their chainsaws, and when a workman cut the highest branch off the tree, the afternoon sun, previously hidden by the branches, poured through the window onto our faces. We were stunned by the glare and by the absence of our wonderful tree. We both started to tear up when the last part of the tree trunk hit the ground. Anne asked, "Daddy, will they cut Mr. Tree now? I don't want them to do that." I said, "No, honey, Mr. Tree is okay. He won't be going away. And we will plant a new tree on the boulevard. You can help me pick it out." She nodded and we walked to the back of the house to make sure that Mr. Tree was okay.

Even as Anne became more independent and creative, she also grew more affectionate, supportive, and sensitive to feelings. One day she gave me a huge hug. I asked her, "How come you gave me that terrific hug?"

She said, "I hugged you because you're such a good daddy. My daddy."

One morning, before the start of school, Billy watched a TV show for too long. He grew anxious and said, "Now I'm going to be late. We won't get there on time at all." He started to cry.

Anne said to me, "Billy sad?"

"Yes, he is."

"Billy sad all day?"

"I don't know. Why don't you ask him?"

"Billy, you sad all day?"

"No, Anne, not all day."

"Oh, goody! Yay." She clapped her hands and smiled.

Anne and her friend Beth, who lived across the street and was just one year older, played together often. One Saturday, Beth's dad came to our front door and asked whether his daughter could stay with us for a while. He was taking Beth's mom to the hospital to have their second child. After he left, Beth began to cry. She missed her parents. Anne put her arms around Beth's shoulders and said, "It's okay, Beth. We will take care of you."

One night at bedtime, Anne said, "Daddy, I want to marry you."

"That's nice of you to say that, but you should marry someone else," I told her.

"No, I love you."

"You can't marry me. I'm your daddy. When you grow up, you'll meet a nice boy, and probably a lot of them."

"You are a nice boy."

"Anne, there will be lots of boys who will come over and want to be your friend. You'll probably marry one of them."

"Maybe you're right, Daddy."

But even this sweet, happy child who had never known her mother was not immune to Sue's death. One night I awoke about 3:00 a.m. to Anne's cries. I went into her bedroom and found her standing up in her bed, blankets strewn aside, tears in her eyes and running down her cheeks. She said, "Why did my mommy have to die?" I held her in my arms as she cried, her little body against my chest. After a long while, she fell back to sleep, still standing. I laid her down and covered her, holding one of her hands as I sat on her bed. The next day, she didn't remember that she had awakened or had cried about her mother's death. For the first time, I realized that the currents ran deep in her, too.

At the same time that Anne's outgoing personality was emerging, Billy became more expressive, more spontaneous; he talked more and seemed happier. With his friends Zac and Andy, he rode his bicycle all over the neighborhood, especially to Lake Harriet and the 7-Eleven store a few blocks away. Calling themselves the Colfax Angels, the boys put playing cards in their bike wheels that noisily announced their presence—which I found reassuring. It's always good to know where your kids are.

Once, before I could stop him, Billy roller-skated in the house, showing off his moves. He was preparing himself for regular visits to the Roller Garden and Saints North roller rink in nearby suburbs, where schoolmates would join him and where we held one of his birthday parties. He collected football and baseball cards and sold a few, building collections he kept for years. He enjoyed summer arts classes. He went fishing in northern Minnesota with Ad and Irene and their friends. His world enlarged. He was "coming back."

Eldora noticed the changes, too. She commented to me once, with what I thought was pride and relief, "He talks much more with me now when he comes home from school. He shows me his work. He lets me comb his hair. It's getting so good. It's so much better this spring, especially in the last few months."

"It sounds as if he's finally accepting you," I said. She nodded.

I knew that this was not an accident. Eldora had continued to reach out to Billy in many ways. She took him and Anne to her home on school holidays and for late-afternoon visits. They cooked, played board games, and walked to nearby Silver Lake. She was always open and friendly to Andy and Zac when they played with him. She sometimes joined us for family birthdays and events.

Eldora was a predictable, friendly presence in Billy's life, someone—unlike earlier nannies—he could depend on. Much later, he told me that she was like another grandmother to him. He found her fun to be around. But he said he still didn't get too attached to her because he knew she was going to leave eventually.

Billy and I spent time together, too. I introduced him to modeling clay figures, something Jim had done for me. We'd figure out a scene or event we wanted to replicate, usually from history. One time we decided to build a couple of Roman galley ships with their crews. Out of clay we made little star figures, flattening one of their sides as heads. With pin pricks on their faces, we gave them eyes and mouths. We added armor, plumed helmets, and pins for their swords. We made dozens and dozens of these guys. We thought we needed two boats—kind of a tough job. We used clay to fashion hulls, made Tinkertoy posts into masts, and created sails out of paper. We put wax paper on the bottoms of the ships and placed them on wooden pegs in a pail of water to get the real effect. It took us many nights to finish the job. For long stretches, Billy played with the boats and their crews. I was glad to have been his partner in this unique project.

Billy didn't watch a lot of TV. He had his favorite weekday-afternoon and Saturday-morning cartoon shows and, with Ad or me, watched the Minnesota Vikings games during football season, but not much beyond that. He preferred to draw pictures or play with his toys. Because he was older than Anne and stayed up later than she did, he and I sometimes watched evening programs or movies. *Hill Street Blues*, starring the former Minnesota Viking Ed Marinaro, was the only show we regularly watched together.

One new television program that he and I also watched together was the miniseries *Roots*, whose episodes were telecast eight nights in a row. Billy asked me many questions: "Why do the Ku Klux Klan come out at night? Why do they wear white sheets? Why are their hats pointed? Why do they have those crosses? Why are they trying to hurt that black man? Why are the white people so bad to the black people? Are those people still around? Black people don't work for whites only, do they?" He told me that once at school a white kid had kicked a black kid and the black kid hit him in retaliation, but mostly all the kids got along.

Watching the series helped Billy and me better understand the historical experience of African Americans. I answered some of his questions, but, since the shows ended at his bedtime, I didn't go into detail. That would come later.

Watching *Roots* promoted conversation between Billy and me about race relations. Another television program, *Eight Is Enough*, prompted a meaningful conversation between Anne and me about other issues, as little as she was. In one episode, the mother and father, who had been single parents before they remarried, shared memories about their former spouses. The wife had gone to a carnival, where she had a conversation with a man who had seen her former husband die in a prisoner of war camp. The husband returned to a cemetery to visit his former wife's grave. Both recalled that there hadn't been enough time to say goodbye to their respective spouses.

When the episode ended, just before Anne's bedtime, she got off my lap, stepped onto the floor, and turned to me with what I thought was a curious look on her face.

"Did you say goodbye to Momma Sue?" she asked.

"Yes, after Momma Sue died, we took her ashes in a plane high above the ocean near Grandpa Bob's cottage in Maine, a place she loved. When I poured out the ashes over the ocean, I said goodbye to Sue. That was the way we did it."

"Were you sad, Daddy?"

"Yes, I was very sad."

"Did you cry?"

"Yes, I did."

"Why?"

"Because I loved Momma Sue very much, but she had died, and she was not coming back. I missed her and felt bad that she wasn't coming back."

When I said that, Anne's face began to fall apart. She suddenly looked years older than four. Very slowly, she started to cry, then reached up and put both of her arms around my neck. We hugged.

"Momma Sue loved you very much," I told her. "When you were a baby, she would hold you in her arms, close to her, rocking you if she was in the rocking chair, never letting you go. She wanted to welcome you to our house, to us. She was proud of you."

As Anne walked quietly down the hallway toward her bedroom, I heard her say, "When I was a little baby, my momma held me all the time." In bed, she asked me, "What are ashes?"

"After people die, we can either put their whole bodies under the ground, where they stay, or make them into fine, little flakes called ashes that go into a box or a jar for keeping or for dropping into a special place, like a park or a lake or the ocean, like we did with Momma Sue."

"Why did you do that?"

"Because she told me that was what she wanted done. And I did it."

"Maybe I'll be flakes, maybe like snowflakes. They go away, too."

I wished Sue had been alive to see Anne and Billy grow up. I knew she would have been proud of them, as I was. She wanted them to succeed in every way possible. I was there, but I often thought how much better their lives would have been if she and I could have parented them together—if each day, after school and outside activities, they could have come home to both of us.

CHAPTER 12

Unrecognized Privileges

❄ ❄ ❄

The kids and I benefited from living in our close-knit neighborhood. For years, the kindness, generosity, and hospitality of my neighbors helped nurture and support us. I was grateful that we could easily access beautiful lakes and parks and that our community was very safe; it had one of the lowest crime rates in Minneapolis. We were close to schools we liked, and our home met our needs. Other public services—healthcare, libraries— were top-notch.

But we paid a price for our neighborhood privileges, as helpful as they were: we interacted almost exclusively with those who shared our culture, class, and lifestyle, hardly any of whom were people of color. We didn't experience the benefits of living in a diverse environment, of stepping beyond our limited perspectives to grow as persons and as citizens.

I did not have a single friend or acquaintance who was a person of color, nor had I while growing up in St. Paul. My childhood neighborhood consisted of white Catholic families, either German, Irish, Italian, or Polish. No people of color lived there or went to my elementary or high schools. None owned or worked in my local drugstore, barbershop, meat market, café, or movie theater, either. They lived in other parts of the city, neighborhoods to which I never went.

The single meaningful interaction I had with people of color as a young person occurred when I was nineteen, playing football for St. John's University of Minnesota against Prairie View A&M from southern Texas. Our team was entirely white and theirs entirely black. We were facing off in the Camellia Bowl, the small-college national championship game in Sacramento, California.

The game occurred in 1963, a time of convulsive changes in America, about six months before the passage of the federal Civil Rights Act. In that era, black athletes played chiefly for historically black colleges and universities—Southern, Grambling, Florida A&M, and Prairie View among them—because major universities in the South had not yet integrated their athletic teams.

Most of us on the field, both black and white, had never played against a team exclusively made up of players of another race. We whites had had almost no contact with black people in our lives, and Prairie View's black players had interacted with whites under the restrictions of segregated policies. In the beginning of the game, it felt surreal: who were these guys? But then we played through a very close, competitive game, which we won. After the game, players on both sides nodded to each other, patted hands or shoulders, or complimented each other. The usual friendly aftermath of any other game.

At the evening banquet, organizers alternated members from each team on both sides of the tables, white and black, black and white. I had to talk to someone on either side or across from me who was not a teammate. As the evening went on, we told each other stories about our coaches, our families, how we got into football, what college was like. Nothing really long—just snippets—but stories I remembered.

The next day, both teams traveled on the same buses from Sacramento to San Francisco for a sightseeing tour of the wharf area. After we got off the buses, clusters of players from both teams walked together, many talking and gesturing, as seagulls swooped above us and a huge group of brown sea lions barked from their wooden platform in the water by the wharf. Most of us had never seen such a sight and laughed as we looked at the animals.

Over that weekend, I got to know people who were different from me and whom I found I liked. But that connection was not deep, nor did it last very long. When our football experience was over, we went back to our segregated environments, typical of the early 1960s at St. John's, in St. Paul, and in the United States.

While my kids were growing up, we lived a lifestyle dominated by our relationships and contacts with white people. They were our neighbors, the owners and employees of our local stores, the staff of our libraries and healthcare services, the people who used our beaches, even the folks who walked our sidewalks, biked on our lake paths, and drove our streets. And they were my colleagues at work, too. It was only in our public schools and playground activities that white people and people of color interacted with each other. But, for the most part, when school days and playground activities ended, people of color left our white neighborhood for other parts of Minneapolis where they lived.

I didn't question this reality. Indeed, I hardly thought about it. It was simply the way things were—just as they had been in my childhood. Much later, I learned why, in part, this was so: until the 1960s, most Minneapolis real estate developers routinely inserted language in mortgage deeds that barred people of color from owning or leasing property in areas throughout the city, especially those near lakes and parks. Local banks, property owners, and public officials, including Federal Housing Administration lenders, accepted this practice, which was known as using racially restrictive deeds or covenants. It is very probable that our home was at one time covered by such a deed, although it was not at the time we purchased it. Given our location near the city's lakes, houses in our area tended to appreciate over time, putting them beyond the financial means of many people of color. It was no accident that our neighborhood was nearly exclusively white.

We also benefited from higher spending on the public services that made our neighborhood so appealing—higher than those in less affluent neighborhoods, where many people of color lived. When budget priorities were decided, local politics worked to our advantage. And we had no issues with police officers. To a considerable extent, the benefits we experienced in our community occurred at the expense of others in our city.

While the kids were small, I did little to introduce them to children or adults who were different from us in or out of our neighborhood. As a single parent, I created and tried to manage a complex daily schedule, one with little flexibility. I didn't seek friendships for myself with many people either, choosing instead to chiefly be with family members and neighbors. I was involved very little in community or political activities that attracted diverse participants. We weren't churchgoers, either. I felt I was living a demanding and full life. I didn't see our neighborhood isolation as a problem for the kids or for me.

Secure in our environment, I didn't experience the economic and political challenges that people of color in North and South Minneapolis—some of them single parents—faced every day. I only occasionally learned about them through media stories.

Being a single dad was hard for me. However, it never occurred to me how much harder it must have been for single parents of color who coped with challenges like mine on top of many more resulting from discriminatory policies and traditions—ones in place specifically because these folks, my fellow citizens, were people of color.

Later, chiefly through participation in some of Billy's and Anne's activities when they were teenagers, I met and made friends with people of color. I worked with them to create a more welcoming environment in our neighborhood schools and parks. But it took a long time before I recognized the advantages we had that were denied to others and did something about it.

While a single parent, I gradually changed my perspectives on many issues: what it means to be a committed father and supportive husband, how to find work/life balance, how to build lifelong friendships, and, most challenging of all, how we as a white family enjoyed certain privileges and the factors that kept them in place.

I realize now the value of my experiences with the Prairie View football players, as limited as they were. Over one weekend, I connected for the first time in a real way with black people in a very physical sport, in conversations, in shared activities. I went beyond the pictures I had seen on television and in the movies or the voices I heard on radio or records. What happened to black Americans while I was in college became important to me, especially as civil rights protests, violence, and eventually federal legislation emerged.

But for more than a decade as a single parent, I was not engaged in the harder effort of improving race relations at the local level. The powerful pull—the benefits—of being in a white community kept me in place. I needed to reconnect on a personal level again with people of color to eventually move beyond that pull. And that didn't come until later.

CHAPTER 13

The Grad School Grind

❋ ❋ ❋

Anne was now old enough for preschool. I scouted local schools, places that I heard had fine programs and wouldn't involve a long drive for Eldora and Anne. I talked with school principals, visited with teachers, scanned classrooms, facilities, and grounds, and compared tuition. The inquiry took time, but I felt good selecting a program at St. Mary's Greek Orthodox Church, which was about a mile from our house.

In Anne's first year, she was in a play with the other preschoolers on a stage in the school's auditorium. I dressed her in a white blouse, blue corduroy skirt and jacket, white socks, and polished black shoes. With a blue ribbon in her hair, she looked proud.

During the performance of three songs, she stood tall, moved to the music, and sang energetically. Most of the other small kids seemed to lose their way; some sat down and never sang, and a few sobbed uncontrollably. My heart went out to these little ones, whose behavior was easy to understand. But I felt a tear of my own coming as I watched Anne onstage, wishing that Sue could have seen her little girl more than holding her own.

The next year we found Especially for Children, a preschool and kindergarten three blocks from our house where both daytime and after-school programs were available. Each day Eldora or I took Anne there in the morning and picked her up in the afternoon. With good teachers, Anne moved through her early school years with ease and seemed ready for first grade when the time came.

She and I shared many favorite activities. One was going to zoos, whether the Como Zoo in St. Paul or the Minnesota Zoo in Apple Valley, a Minneapolis suburb. She liked animals, so we made many trips to both. Once when we watched a male tiger stride impatiently back and forth for a long time, Anne asked, "Daddy, do you think he is lonely? He doesn't look very happy."

"He could be hungry, too," I said. "But you could be right. He's got a big area to be in, but he seems to be all by himself." I wasn't sure my answer satisfied Anne, but it was a typical question from her—she connected to feelings, human or otherwise.

She also liked riding on the small train cars that ran on a large circular track. She frequently sat alone, head tilted slightly, smiling, as she felt the breeze blowing her hair. I thought she seemed comfortable in herself.

During that period, I took Billy to the airport for a one-week trip on his own to see Grandpa Bob in Los Angeles. With his hair parted down the middle, mod fashion, he looked older than his age. We talked for a while about what he and Bob would do and boarded the plane together. Once he was seated, I gave him a hug.

"I think you better go now, Dad. I want to be alone," he said. As I walked up the aisle of the plane, he called out, "Wave to me from the terminal, Dad!" When the huge Western Airlines jet left the runway and started its ascent, the symbolism was too much to miss: I was reminded that all parents must, at some time, let their children go, and how hard that is to do.

Billy was beginning to grow up—he was not the child he had been when Sue died. From birth to about age five, he, like most other children, had been vulnerable in many ways and needed my close attention. When he moved through the next period of his life, ages five to eleven, he had grown more self-sufficient, more independent, more confident. Traveling by himself on an airplane for a long trip was a sign of his growth and of what was to come.

Once we had Eldora as our permanent nanny, I was able to return to my PhD program. Over a three-year period, I researched, wrote, and defended my dissertation, which was a research study on budgetary decision-making in public universities. Leaders at my university's central administration were interested in my research. They approved several short unpaid leaves of absence for me and allowed me once to dip into my retirement funds to offset my loss of pay. On one occasion, a vice president transferred funds to my office to cover leave costs. I was grateful for their support. It gave me the opportunity to both finish graduate school and meet our family expenses on a single salary, a challenge for most single parents—male and female—that I met.

Billy and Anne's local grandparents helped me by caring for the children on weekends so I could work on my research. Some weeks, Mom stayed with us both Friday and Saturday; on most other weekends, Ad and Irene took the kids Sunday morning and early afternoon so I could work at my campus office, where I had all my materials.

One summer, I spent nine days straight at our Mekenok Island cabin, drafting several chapters, while the three grandparents and their friends covered for me. I was grateful for their support. Even with their help, much of the time it felt like a long haul—combining work for pay during the day with dissertation research at night or on weekends for three years until I graduated.

The path wasn't always smooth. My faculty advisors were slow to read chapters I had written. Sometimes three or four weeks would pass before I got a response—a phone call or chapter edits—from one of them. The review process seemed unpredictable to me and stressed me out.

Some days, I couldn't find the energy to write. Ongoing needs—making meals, doing the laundry, creating activity schedules for the kids—interfered. On some occasions, I slowed down or stopped what I was doing and vividly remembered my experiences with Sue, both good and challenging. On one Saturday, after I dropped the kids at Irene's and Ad's home in St. Paul, I drove to the apartment where Sue lived while she was in graduate school, near the University of Minnesota's Minneapolis campus.

Her building was across the street from the Mississippi River, which was partially hidden by trees on a path we walked many times. Snow was on the ground, but the river was flowing and the sun was bright. I walked into her building—security hadn't become a necessity then—and up the stairs to her apartment, number 207. I stood by the door, feeling an aura, an atmosphere of warmth and friendship, the same feeling I had had when

I returned from my work in Florida for a reunion with her. Other memories about her apartment came back. The many times we had hosted dinners and parties for friends and family, conversations we had with other graduate students, my overnight stays. She made me my first oven-baked, open-faced tuna fish sandwich: tuna, mayo, celery, and a slice of tomato, topped with melted yellow cheddar cheese. It was delicious. Standing in the hallway, I could taste it.

I walked back to my car, feeling better but confused. What I was missing, in the face of the seemingly endless PhD work, the single parenting, and my job, was Sue—as a companion, a partner. I remembered her last card to me. On the front, a large white dog stands close to a small blue bird that has a red ribbon on its head. The dog is holding one of its floppy ears over the bird to protect it from falling rain. Inside, the preprinted message reads, "You are my sunshine." Sue added her own note: "And you are! You and Billy are the most wonderful things that ever happened to me, and I treasure you. Love, Sue."

That Saturday, I opened a door. I went to the place where my feelings took me. I wasn't feeling treasured, but I relived an experience worth remembering. It often was like that: no periods of grief or depression or haunting dreams about her, but rather a tape running soundlessly through my head—one whose arrival was unpredictable but one I couldn't ignore. As the years passed, some of my memories of her and our life faded a bit, but others remained vivid.

During this graduate school period, I also experienced a setback of my own doing. After I had finished my dissertation and passed my final oral examination before a faculty committee, but before I graduated, my chief advisor suggested I prepare a presentation for a regional conference in higher education that was being held locally. It would be a good experience for me to prepare and deliver a paper in a professional setting—it would help me practice needed presentation skills, could get me known in a network of professionals, and might lead to job opportunities.

I was excited at his suggestion and submitted a presentation proposal, which was accepted. I was given a 6:30 p.m. time slot at the end of the daylong conference, which began at 8:00 a.m. Being that late in the program was the worst possible slot, but, as a graduate student, I didn't expect better treatment. Senior scholars and administrators got top billing. I was glad to have cracked the lineup at all.

The night before my presentation, Billy and Anne both got sick. Billy had a cold and needed cough medicine twice during the night, and on two occasions Anne was restless and crying from something I never discovered. Even though I only got about four hours of sleep, I felt good when the conference started—buoyed by adrenaline. But as the day wore on, and the effects of my 11:30 lunch faded, my energy disappeared. I hadn't had any snacks during the day, either, and few liquids.

When I stood up to begin my presentation, I felt shaky, the audience members seemed to be floating away from me, and my words disappeared as I spoke. I saw looks of concern and furrowed brows on the faces in front of me. Then I fainted. I was told later that my head missed the wooden podium by only a few inches. I remember only starting to fall, and then I was on the floor.

People ran to me, one helped me to sit up, another gave me a paper cup of water, and two others helped me stand and guided me to a seat in the front row. There was a hush in the crowd. I looked up to see faces staring at me, a few whispering to each other. I was embarrassed. I felt like such a failure.

After a rest, I decided to deliver the presentation and read carefully from my notes. When I finished, there was no applause. The audience just left. No faculty members or graduate students from my college visited with me. It was a terrible first experience, but I learned a couple of important lessons: always prepare as if something unexpected might go wrong, and be sure to have a water bottle and snacks. Self-evident insights, but ones I had to learn through experience.

Eventually, I did graduate, walking in academic robes to collect my diploma. My family attended the ceremony and afterward held a party for me. Anne cut tiny pieces of cake for the guests. Billy said, "You did a good job, Dad, but you should have smiled when you were walking up front in the auditorium. We all waved at you, too, but you didn't seem to see us."

Billy was right. I hadn't seen them at all. I was in a daze, thinking, *Is this really over? Am I finished?* The doctoral program had lasted seven years (with interruptions), a big part of my adult life. I didn't know what would come next in terms of work or even in other aspects of my life. With the PhD in hand, though, I hoped new work opportunities would arise.

While I was in graduate school, I had a stable job, with good fringe benefits, but we were living paycheck to paycheck. My salary covered childcare pay for Eldora, occasional after-school classes for Billy, and our ongoing family expenses. Our Ford Pinto wagon ran okay, but paying for any unexpected repairs was a challenge. We had access to a free summer vacation cabin, for which I was grateful. I put money into reunion travels with Bob in Los Angeles or Maine during the summers and Ad and Irene in Tucson, Arizona, when they wintered there, which I viewed as a priority. Many years, though, my credit card bills neared my salary. I couldn't save enough to meet down payment and monthly mortgage payment requirements for our house. Very high mortgage interest rates, which ran 17 to 18 percent in that period, didn't help. So we rented from Ad and Irene. I felt a little discouraged but didn't see a way to change things all that quickly, especially when I was in graduate school with a full schedule and little opportunity to increase my income.

I met other single parents at the children's schools or at park activities or at work. We talked about how much we were "having it all." We'd say, "Should we change places with all those happily married couples?" The typical answer was "You bet," especially for women who couldn't find full- or part-time work with an adequate salary and benefits and who often coped with demanding childcare and sometimes also eldercare responsibilities. In comparison to them, I was advantaged, given the job, finances, health, and family support I had.

But the question of "Can you have work and family life balance?" never quite went away. Colleagues at the university, especially those without children, worked longer hours than I did. They built relationships with senior leaders and managers that eventually led to promotions. I relieved Eldora at 5:00 p.m. sharp and couldn't build those social relationships at the office or with others in professional networks who knew about new or expanded job opportunities or might have become mentors.

For me and other single parents, finding the time and energy needed to parent our children and work for pay outside the home was never a given. A sickness, an accident, an appliance that broke down, a snowstorm that snarled transportation—all undercut stability, momentum, and even confidence in handling everyday life needs and experiences. The feeling of scrambling with the unexpected never really went away, nor did the reality that I was "it": my children's last line of defense. I made the key decisions in their lives, whether or not I had the information or time I thought I needed or the outside support.

I was sometimes scared of failing. The self-rating system I created was brutal, too: "I screwed up," "I could have done better," "No one else would be that dumb!" my inner critic would say. All the single parents I knew, including me, pointed to experiences they wished they could have avoided, decisions they wished they could have made with the help of a partner. We did our best and hoped that we and our children had the resilience to make it through hard times. And we kept looking for ways to make our lives better.

Sue and I on our wedding day, August 6, 1969

From left to right, the Hoebel family— Cindy, Bart, Brett, (Grandpa) Ad, Val, (Granny) Irene, Cary—and Sue, Billy, and me at our Mekenok Island cabin

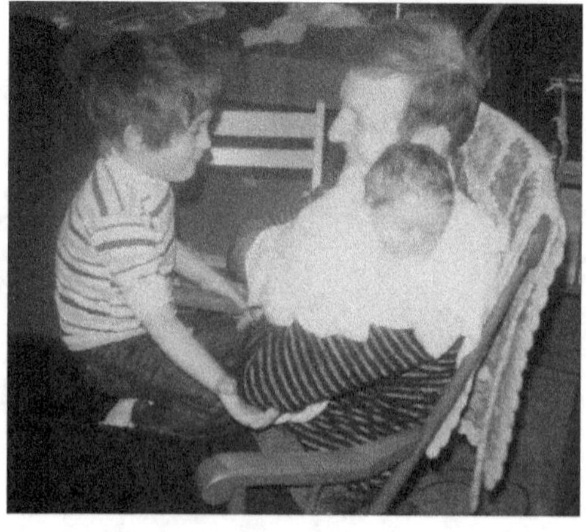

I loved rocking baby Anne and Billy, too, when he joined us.

Our last picture of Sue before
she died on Easter Sunday,
April 18, 1976

Anne, five months old;
Billy, five years old; and
me at the cabin

Billy teaching Anne
how to make good
music

Three sleepy travelers after a full vacation day in Ocean Park, Maine

Andy and Zac, neighborhood buddies, with Billy

From left to right, four generations of Delmont fellas: my Grandpa Nick; my dad, Jimmy; my brother, Jim; my nephew, David; Billy; and me

Ready to take out presents
from the Christmas stockings
knitted by Granny Irene

We three posing
for our 1978
Christmas card

Identical jammies for
Christmas Eve

Ready for Halloween

Billy showing Anne
the way

When I finished my PhD,
we had a great party.

CHAPTER 14

A Missing Dad

※ ※ ※

One of the challenges of being a single parent is deciding on which relationships to build and sustain. There is never enough time to reach out to all the family and friends with whom we might have intimate or even casual relationships. The children and I had abiding bonds with their grandparents on Sue's side, my mom, and some friends and neighbors, but not with my dad, Jimmy.

Dad was in many ways a remarkable person. He had been a star in three high school sports. His high school basketball team won the Minnesota state championship. He was voted the most valuable player on the all-state tournament team. He had been a college football and baseball player and played professional baseball up to the Triple-A level, one below the major leagues. If it hadn't been for a knee injury, he very likely could have made the big leagues.

He published a biography of Floyd B. Olson, Minnesota's most famous governor during the Great Depression. As a radio broadcaster in the Twin Cities, Dad had the highest-rated show during evening rush hour as well as a popular late-night radio program. He also hosted a Sunday-morning sports television program, for which pilots were made for national television syndication. He was a gregarious, humorous, highly intelligent, warm man, in the best sense a local celebrity who was recognized and welcomed wherever he went in public.

Following my parents' divorce, Dad regularly spent Saturday afternoons with my brother and me. He took us fishing, to movies, and to University of Minnesota football games and Harlem Globetrotters basketball games. He was an affectionate, attendant father, the kind who threw his arm around my shoulders while we were seated in a movie theater. More than once while broadcasting, he would dedicate songs to me when I was sick at home from school. "This song is for my son Timmy, who is not feeling well today. Hope you enjoy it, son," he'd say. I loved that.

By the time I was about eight, however, the visits stopped as a second marriage, his work, and an increasing addiction to alcohol captured his weekends. Through my elementary school, high school, college, and post-college years, he was a phantom parent. Later, Sue and I would invite him to dinner, but he never came, although he worked in the Twin Cities Monday through Friday.

After Billy and Anne were born, Dad initiated little contact with them, although he sometimes sent gift money for Christmas. Billy's childhood letters to him went unanswered. In one, Billy wrote that he was small for his age: "The doctors we have seen say I'll grow more in high school and I'll be bigger than the next guy. I would really like to play quarterback in high school, but who needs a shrimp?" That one begged for a response from his grandpa, a former quarterback, but it didn't come.

Building a relationship with him was a challenge. He lived with his second wife, Gladie, and my half-brother, John, and half-sister, Laurie, in Los Angeles. On one trip out there, while the kids and I were staying with Bob, we visited with my dad and his family. We had a good time, but otherwise nothing changed in our relationship. We didn't stay in close contact.

The next year, on another visit with Bob, I invited Dad and Bob to lunch so we could get to know one another better. Dad began drinking martinis during our conversation and, after a few drinks, passed out. His face hit the tabletop and glasses and dishes broke, scattered in the air, and fell to the floor. Bob and I were stunned. Other customers stared at us.

We lifted Dad upright, checked to see whether he was bleeding, and offered him some water. He was slow to respond and become fully conscious. We thought we would take him home in Bob's car, but when we tried to help him walk, he couldn't stand. He was so heavy that we couldn't hold him up. We called a cab, and the driver helped us get him into it. We knew that the caretaker or friends at Dad's apartment would help take him to his place once he arrived.

Dad was on some kind of medication, but, as far as I knew, he had passed out from drinking. That was a deciding experience for me—what little trust I had in him was now gone. After that, I didn't try to continue a relationship between the kids and him, nor did he. I also didn't reach out to his dad, my grandpa Nick, who was alive and healthy and living in St. Paul.

After my parents divorced, Nick hadn't been in much contact with my mom, my brother, or me. My kids and I very likely missed some important experiences with Dad, his second family, and Nick and his wife. But I intentionally prioritized my relationships with the grandparents who had been there for us before and after Sue's death over the family members who didn't make much of an effort. I was sad about having to make that decision, but I didn't doubt it was the right one. I went where the payoff was best for Billy and Anne.

Many years later, after my dad died, I took a course offered by the Landmark Forum, a training institute, created to help adults improve their relationships with family members and others. One exercise we were asked to complete was to write a letter to someone important in our lives with whom we had an underdeveloped, incomplete, or unhappy relationship. It could be a letter of forgiveness for wrongs done, acceptance of losses felt, or thanks for what had been given us. I chose to write several letters to family members, including one to my dad.

When I started writing, I thought the letter would be very short. I was surprised when it easily went to two pages, single spaced. He had affected me more than I had realized, often in positive ways. My letter, in part, said:

> For most of my life, you have seemed a phantom to me, appearing most often when I was a small boy, emerging on rare occasions when I was a teenager, and disappearing nearly completely when I was an adult. I was acquainted with you, but I really didn't know you.

I feel bad that we never built a significant relationship of father and son, that we shared so little in common, and that we had so little time together.

I am writing to tell you that I forgive you for not being the father of my expectations and to thank you for things that you did give me, some of which I have used as a parent with Billy and Anne.

I thanked him for his abilities and accomplishments in athletics, warmth and ease with people, commitment to hard work and self-sufficiency, sharing of our connection to the family's Italian heritage, and communication skills.

I finished the letter: "I now know that you did the best you could, that a second marriage and your battle with alcoholism pulled you away from me. You didn't give me a lot of what I wanted, but you did give me important things of lasting value. I am grateful for them and I promise to use the gifts I've gained from you to better my life and the lives of my family members and friends."

I don't know whether I would have mailed this letter to my dad if he had still been alive. But writing it lifted a burden and assuaged a sense of loss and disappointment about our relationship. I felt I was still my father's son, even though we were very different people.

CHAPTER 15

Dating Again

⚹ ⚹ ⚹

I don't remember when I started to feel like dating again. It just happened. I accompanied a friend to a church service where, over coffee, I met a preschool teacher who was the divorced mother of three teenagers. We went on a few dates before she said, "I like you, Tim, and I think something might really grow between us. But I'm thirty-nine with three kids, a couple headed to college soon. I just can't deal with a baby anymore." It hadn't occurred to me that my having a baby would be a roadblock in developing a relationship with someone new—though it probably should have.

When I began dating, I held certain expectations. I was looking for someone who had a similar educational and cultural background to mine, was professionally employed, and shared at least some of my interests in politics, leisure activities, and the arts—predictable characteristics. I was attracted to women who had intelligence, warmth, friendliness, a sense of humor, and a certain physical look: tall, with long brown hair, pretty, like many folk singers of the 1960s.

I was also looking for someone I perceived as a strong person, a characteristic I valued highly. I was raised by a mom who had strength, one who, in the 1940s, visited a psychiatrist for marriage advice when hardly anyone in her family or community did; who divorced an abusive husband when few Catholic women ever did; who in middle age taught herself how to type, practicing persistently, to get a full-time job when nearly all moms were homemakers; and who managed a five-person family of three generations on a modest income.

I expected the women I dated to be her match, as I thought Sue had been. Sue had many strengths, including a willingness to work hard, a capacity for sharing and partnering, empathy for others, and maturity. I wanted to find someone who, like her, was easily my equal or more and who, because of that, would help me grow, help me become a better person and parent.

What Sue and I had discovered was that we each had limitations that worked against the success of our marriage. We knew less than we thought we did about promoting compatibility, using financial resources prudently, or raising small children. Mutual physical attraction wore thin. It took therapy individually and together to build understanding and skills—especially in communication and conflict management—that would help us become better companions and partners, to be better matched as a couple. But I didn't have much time after Anne was born to practice with Sue what we had learned about how to make a relationship work.

When I started dating regularly again, I met some women who had had miserable, even traumatic, experiences with their husbands or partners. They and their children had survived physical and emotional abuse, alcohol- and drug-related behaviors, the squandering of financial resources, and desertion. Somehow, they got by, but building a romantic relationship couldn't or wouldn't be a priority. Their confidence and trust in men might emerge again, but it would take time for them to rebuild, if they ever did.

Some shared their stories with me, while others only hinted at their shattering experiences or generally difficult lives. I thought we might have a chance to build something good, even lasting. But when those relationships failed to materialize, I thought I could see why.

My mom had been one of those women who experienced abuse and then divorce and didn't remarry or, as far as I knew, even date again. But she had successfully raised Jim and me. I had benefited from her decision to go it alone. I was reminded by her example how dedicated—even heroic—these women were as single parents, meeting their obligations each day without a partner. My dad had been abusive, and I had seen the continuing negative impact of his behavior on my mom and our family. As parents, they had very different track records.

Some of the women I dated were committed to building their careers and had very little time or interest in a serious relationship, or at least one with me. Job opportunities were opening up for professional women that previously had been closed to them. I thought the impact of the emerging women's movement on the work and lives of huge numbers of American women—opening doors that had been closed—was enormously positive. I hadn't anticipated that it would lead some women in my age bracket to value their jobs over dating and romantic relationships. One woman I dated briefly said, "You know, I don't have the time I wish I had. There is so much to do at work. I'm sorry."

Once I had planned a lunch date with a woman I had met. I waited for an hour at the restaurant, but she never showed up, nor did she answer her phone when I called her from a pay phone on the street. I was more disappointed and confused than angry. *What's going on here?* I thought. When I reached her that evening, she told me that something had come up, without offering much of an apology. I chalked up rejections to typical dating brush-offs—there was nothing irresistible about me. But I noticed an emerging pattern: single women were not as focused on dating and ultimately finding a husband as they had been in the past.

As a result, my dating history was filled with starts and stops. I seemed to be good at getting initial interest but not at keeping things going. I had issues with women and they with me. It would take me more time and more dating to understand how my attitudes and behaviors sometimes undercut my relationships. In the early years after Sue's death, my self-awareness, while growing, was still modest.

Eventually I realized that I needed to value and engage more fully in the emotional life of my relationships. I started to recognize some of my limitations: Being overly rational and analytical far too often. Not listening effectively. Repressing my feelings or being unwilling to share or examine them. Being judgmental about behaviors or conflicts. It wasn't a short list. I often unthinkingly reflected the dominant male culture in which I was raised. Some women I dated let me know that I had a ways to go.

There was much, however, that was positive in my dating experiences. I was surprised by how easy it was to meet women—easier than I had expected. I met them at preschool and elementary school activities, playgrounds, church services, neighborhood block parties, and university events. Friends and family members made regular offers to arrange dates for me, some of which I accepted. They'd even babysit, sometimes on short notice. On several occasions, women called me for a date. That was easy to take and something that hardly ever happened when I was dating in the 1960s.

While Billy and Anne were small, I met a lot of women. After spending countless hours with little people, being with another adult in a fun or romantic situation was such a relief! And finding someone who seemed to like or care about me was a wonderful boost. The notion that I counted, at least at this time in the eyes of this woman, was real and important.

I did sustain a number of relationships over many months or longer. I found mutual attraction and real companionship, if not love and a commitment to marriage. I learned to value friendships that had elements of romance and caring, relationships that ended when one of us wanted to find someone with whom we could develop a serious relationship with a good chance of marriage.

I was also surprised that sex seemed to happen easily. Most of the women I dated were also single parents and, like me, didn't have exclusive partners. We seemed to share a "let's take the moment" attitude: we both knew loneliness, and sex offered physical and emotional connection, however temporary. It wasn't necessarily linked to whether we loved one another or were considering marriage. It was about feeling fully human when our single-parent lifestyle was an often demanding and sometimes grinding experience. Sex could be something good that transcended the limitations of the relationships.

In the years since I had married Sue, dating norms had changed. Most of the women I dated after her death had professional careers and full agendas as single moms. Some were looking for a serious romance, but many were not. I wanted companionship, and found it, but finding someone to love and marry was much more of a challenge than I had anticipated. And I had work to do to be a better partner for a woman who wanted a romantic relationship with me. But I still thought somebody was out there for me—and for the kids.

CHAPTER 16

Football and More

⋇ ⋇ ⋇

I was standing on the sidelines of the football field. My shoes were coated with mud; rain dripped off my cap. Billy, age ten, ran toward me as the game was winding down. He had pulled ahead of many tacklers from the other team and was heading for the goal line. He ran through puddles, splashing water and pieces of mud and grass, right past me. No one caught him.

When he scored the touchdown, all of us on the sidelines were laughing, shouting, and clapping for him and his team—they had won the playoff game and were headed for the next round.

"That kid is really good," one bystander said.

"He'll play high school ball, for sure. Maybe college," said another. I hoped so.

Billy loved to play football; it was the first sport that piqued his interest. The hometown Minnesota Vikings were his team. His Grandpa Ad, Sue's stepfather, read him stories about their players, and the three of us watched their games on Sunday afternoons. For several years, Billy and I drove to Mankato, Minnesota—about ninety miles from Minneapolis—to watch their training camp practices. During one of those drives, six-year-old Billy asked, "Do you think I'll get an autograph today? Or get to talk to one of the guys?" Such anticipation. He was approaching his heroes.

After the Vikings ended their practice and walked off the field, Billy shyly asked these very large guys, who towered over him, to autograph his program, and they did. We drove home past the southern Minnesota farm fields of corn, wheat, and soybeans, his practice program on his lap, reliving our experiences, building a connection around football that would last. I was grateful to be sharing something of importance with him when he was still young.

Football talk between Billy and me about getting in shape, what happened at practices, and how games went ran in the family. As a child, my brother, Jim, had introduced me to the game: we played catch in our yard, went to University of Minnesota Gopher games with our dad, and always listened to their games when they were on the road. My dad and I both played high school and college football. Like Billy, Dad was a quarterback; I was a center, the lineman who snapped the ball to the quarterback. Billy was energized on his football teams, both at practice and in games. He made friends and played hard and well. He found a place and an identity in football and in other sports, as both my dad and I had.

When we came home after his team won the playoff game, he was elated. He headed to our bathroom and was stripping off his muddy gear to shower when our doorbell rang. I answered the door and greeted his three coaches, all high school seniors at Washburn High School in Minneapolis, where Billy wanted to play. They had come to congratulate him on his play and to give him a bronze trophy as the game's most valuable player. When I called him back to see his coaches, he was still half-dressed in his muddy gear. The coaches gave Billy the trophy, patted him on his back and shoulders, and laughed with him.

He continued to play quarterback, improving each year. In high school, he became the starting quarterback for the B squad and moved up to varsity. Then, in his senior year, a leg injury ended his football career. Billy was really disappointed and discouraged about his injury. It was hard to take. In time, he focused on selecting a college, without football as a factor.

Much later when we talked about our football experiences, he said, "Football was wonderful. I loved it. I was a team leader, and I was good at it. There was camaraderie. I learned how to get along and cooperate. You supported me; you knew the game. And I wasn't nervous. Just enjoyed it." Injuries, we agreed, were only part of the story.

Like Billy, Anne was a good athlete. Her first sport was horseback riding, and then came soccer and softball in park league and high school programs at Washburn. Her coaches told me she was a quick learner, something I experienced for myself when I volunteered to coach her middle school softball team. I had practiced football with Billy and watched all his games but hadn't coached any of his teams. I was sad about that but couldn't find a way as a single parent to make our family and my work schedules dovetail. When Anne moved to the middle school level, Billy was in high school and more independent, and I had more flexibility.

I loved every facet of coaching Anne's team, from figuring out how to practice on rain-soaked fields to deciding on what positions each girl would be best at—first base was a great fit for Anne—to doing what I could to build positive relationships among them and between them and me. The principal value I tried to emphasize was respect for what each individual player contributed, a value that had characterized the coaching style of my high school and college football coaches.

I had a few exchanges with my coaches that I never forgot. In the locker room after my final football game for Cretin High School, our line coach, Ted Joyce, sat down next to me. He said very little to any of us during the year—he wasn't a talker. But today, in his quiet way, he leaned over and said, "We are very proud of you, Tim. You made the most improvement of any lineman we've had here. Congratulations." I felt grateful and hardly knew what to say, except to thank him. Mr. Joyce's compliment was a gift to me as a teenager who wasn't so sure of how well he had done. It meant a lot to me, too, because my dad never attended any of my high school games, and my mom had been at only one. I made sure to praise Anne and her teammates when they deserved it, remembering how I felt when Mr. Joyce praised me.

We won most of our softball games, but sometimes my players made mistakes, and unresolved issues at home interfered occasionally with the girls' on-field concentration and decision-making. In those situations, I used an approach my college football coach, John Gagliardi, had modeled.

After I injured my right knee in a game during my senior season, medical staff treated me with a knee-to-ankle cast. As I walked from the infirmary dragging my leg in its cast, John stopped, put his hand on my shoulder, and said, "It pains me to see you this way. Now promise me you'll work really hard to get over this. I want you back on my team." I felt tears in my eyes. At the moment I was feeling the worst, Coach John was there for me—a player who could not be a starter and was not likely to help his team win its remaining games.

John treated me with respect and challenged me to do my best under disheartening circumstances—something I tried to do with Anne and her teammates. I listened as carefully as I could to their problems and helped them come up with solutions. Anne later told me, "Sports was always fun—being with my teammates, my friends, at games and at their houses. I liked having you as my coach. So did the other kids. It was cool." I don't know how good a coach I was, but it felt great to have done it.

As a parent of athletes, I was determined to do for Billy and Anne what my parents had not done for me: Show up. Be engaged. Make their team sports one of my priorities. But there was no soccer mom for Billy and Anne. A very important person would not join me in sharing sports with them. I hoped their coaches, teammates, friends, and members of other families whom they met through sports would help me fill that vacuum. In some ways, they did.

Watching my kids play sports made me remember my own experiences. Hours of running, sprinting, and lifting weights to get in shape for football before two-a-day practices started in August. Perspiration soaking through all my clothes. Being so tired I was hardly able to move.

Playing in a college playoff game at Metropolitan Stadium, the first home of the Vikings, during late November. Snow was on the frozen field; my cleats made sharp clicking sounds with each step I took. Thousands of fans were bundled in snowmobile outfits and parkas, their breaths small puffs in the frigid air. An almost surreal experience. Learning how to live with bruises and nuisance pains while rehabbing injuries throughout long football seasons. I was often anxious, not knowing how quickly I would recover or play again.

In basketball as an eighth grader, turning quickly and lifting a ten-foot shot that won a city playoff game in overtime. When I came out of the gym, a light snow was falling, the moon shone brightly, and I was surrounded by a small crowd clapping and hugging me. So joyous.

In elementary school baseball, endlessly missing curveballs and sliders; strikeouts were embarrassing and hard to remedy. Not a lot of fun. But I loved wearing my baseball uniform in school on game days, walking down the hallways, through the lunchroom, and into the classrooms. A special status.

Sports were a performance art that made demands, resulting in mixed outcomes, all fixed in my memory. Because of sports, I was healthier than I might otherwise have been, I was determined to succeed in a host of activities, and I learned to live with disappointments and rebound from them. Participation in sports stretched me, matured me, helped me develop the attitudes and habits—and the confidence—that I would need when I became a single parent.

Much of what I did as a parent drew from my experience in sports: Respect my kids for who they are. Put their needs before my own. Set expectations. Listen to what they say. Work together. Make timely decisions. Hold them accountable for following family rules. Accept shortcomings, theirs and mine. Do my best, day in and day out.

Family Bonds

✻ ✻ ✻

As Billy and Anne grew older, I asked them to assume more family responsibilities. I thought they were old enough to share our common work and begin building new skills by doing their own laundry, cleaning their rooms and other rooms in the house, and helping wash or dry dishes after meals. We agreed on their chores, for which I gave them an allowance. We started functioning as a three-person family, in cooperation with one another.

With cooperation also came more competition, as Anne was now able to hold her own with her older brother. Like most siblings, they would squabble over all sorts of things: who got which chair, which TV show to watch, whose friends could come over. They could be nasty to each other, too. Once, Anne ran a purple marker over Billy's football cards—his prized possession. Another time, she pulled down small strips of his bedroom wallpaper. He responded by pushing her to the floor and throwing her dolls and clothes around. We had our share of family discussions and time-outs that involved one or both kids.

On occasion, I abandoned my parental peacemaking duties by taking baths during the day or at night, bathroom door tightly locked. Despite the hollering going on outside or the pounding on the bathroom door—"Daddy, come out, you've got to come out! Billy is not fair!"—I slid into the warm bathwater, felt the bubbles that lapped about me, and ignored the noise beyond the door. I would put candles on the four corners of the tub and turn off the lights—tiny red flickers in the darkness and soothing water. It was a wonderful time for rest and relaxation, free from what seemed like twenty-four-hour-a-day duties. Far too soon, these moments would pass and I would have to return to reality, but those warm baths helped me cope.

Another mechanism of escape for me was taking the kids on frequent trips to the downtown Minneapolis YWCA. The Y was close to us, its membership costs were modest, and it was family friendly, with expansive hours and times scheduled for family-only use of the gym and equipment—lots of advantages. On Sunday afternoons, especially in winter when stir-craziness was at its height, I piled Billy and Anne into our station wagon and went to the Y. It didn't give me the privacy of my leisurely baths, but I benefited from the exercise, and I conveniently exhausted both kids in playing kickball, climbing walls, and swimming. Then we'd go home and have supper, and right away my tired children would head to bed, which freed the evening for whatever I wanted to do.

Single parenting bred its own kind of mindlessness, whether too-frequent forgetfulness or silly decision-making. One time Anne was sick, stayed home from school, and mostly spent her days in bed. Eldora called me at work and asked me to pick up some ice cream that Anne had requested. On my way home, I bought the ice cream and some other groceries, then stopped at the shoemaker's for a pair of loafers I had gotten resoled. When I came home, I went upstairs to see how Anne was feeling, told her I had gotten the ice cream, and then went to my bedroom to change my clothes.

Later, while making dinner, I had a strange feeling—something was wrong, something didn't fit, but I didn't know what. I opened the freezer; next to the blue ice cube tray was a finely polished size eleven pair of brown loafers, just a little frosted. I went to my bedroom, opened the closet door, and found a plastic grocery bag on the floor, next to my bedroom slippers. A fine, but discernible, trail of melted vanilla ice cream was working its way onto and past my slippers toward the rest of my shoes. I had to laugh.

I don't know the number of umbrellas, pairs of gloves, stocking caps, pens and pencils, library books, and car keys that I left somewhere only to discover later that they were gone. Once, while putting grocery bags into my car, I set my billfold on the roof. About a block from the store, I remembered what I had done. I did a fast U-turn, returned to the store, and searched the parking lot for the billfold. No luck. I asked the grocery store staff whether anyone had turned in a billfold. Nope. I walked the block from the parking lot to where I had done my turn, carefully searching the street, sometimes on my hands and knees, hoping to find it. Nothing.

When I got home and finished putting the groceries away, I noticed that the light on the answering machine was blinking. The message was from a stranger who had found my billfold in the street after it had blown off my car roof, seen my home address on my driver's license, brought the billfold to my home, and left it in my mailbox for me. He didn't leave his name. I walked quickly out to the mailbox. My wallet was there! Such relief and such generosity by an honest person in Minneapolis. At times only a Good Samaritan could save a single parent like me from myself.

After Anne turned six, she started first grade and full-time school. We no longer needed Eldora or Mom for childcare; it didn't make sense for them to do after-school duty only. Anne had grown more independent, more interested in being with her friends, more confident about participating in after-school activities, whether at her school or our local park.

Eldora had been especially good with Anne when she was a little girl, but she had felt my daughter slipping away. "Tim, she doesn't want to do things with me like she used to," she told me, a wisp of sadness in her voice. Five years had passed, and it was time for Eldora to look for other small children to care for. We had a dinner for her at Ad and Irene's, with presents and hugs, and some tears among the adults.

Decades later, when Eldora died, I went to her memorial service and her family gathering. Her daughter Merrily said, "Mom loved taking care of Billy and Anne. She said that after Daddy died, working with your little ones made her life worthwhile. It was really hard for her to stop, but she was so grateful for the experience and for the way all of you treated her."

"She saved us, you know," I told her. "What she did for my kids, especially Anne, was incredible. I always knew I could trust her. We missed her."

First grade opened the door for Anne to loads of after-school and summer children's activities whose fees we could afford—swimming, gymnastics, cooking and drawing classes, weeklong camps, and horseback riding. I wanted her to experience the same opportunities for growth and development outside of our home that Billy had, to feel confident that she could accomplish things that challenged her. Eldora, the grandmothers, and I had always agreed that we would treat Anne about the same as we did Billy—similar expectations for behaviors, similar personal and family responsibilities, similar consequences for her actions—while allowing for some gender differences.

On one rare occasion, Eldora had proposed to enter Anne in a citywide "Little Princess" contest, in which five-year-old girls outfitted in pink dresses and tiaras competed for the title of prettiest girl. I thought that kind of contest put too much emphasis on looks and nixed it. I saw her as the little girl she was but didn't want to send a signal that we valued her appearance over her many other individual qualities. If there had been a "Little Prince" contest based on good looks when Billy was small, I wouldn't have entered him in that, either.

Of course, it wasn't always smooth sailing. I dropped in at one after-school facility and found it in chaos: some kids were running around unsupervised, swinging jackets at each other. Others were sitting by themselves crying. Food and clothing was strewn across the floor of the room where I found Anne and no teachers or aides were nearby. I withdrew her from that school to find another with adequate programming and supervision. I learned that even in Minneapolis, there were no guarantees about program quality.

Meanwhile, Billy had drawing and sailing lessons, basketball and football camps, and his annual trip with me to watch the Minnesota Vikings at their training camp. He began a once-a-week newspaper route, delivering a neighborhood paper to about a hundred homes in the area where we lived. He used his pay to buy comic books. He never missed a delivery, whatever the weather. I admired his self-sufficiency and, in our neighborhood, knew he was safe.

Before the time of computer spreadsheets, scheduling was its own art. Sometimes Billy helped by posting his schedule on our refrigerator or in his room, but usually I made long lists of day-to-day activities and loaded a large refrigerator calendar with critical times and places. I enrolled the kids in after-school activities at their schools or at parks nearby, where busing was minimal, and drove them in early evenings as needed. I knew they benefited from their experiences in sports, music, and arts programs, but we pushed our limits at times—I often drove one or both of them four or five nights a week to activities.

When some lasted beyond Billy's and Anne's bedtimes, they argued and picked at each other. Sometimes I ran out of energy and patience, too. "Can you two just shut up? What's your problem?" I remember saying to them on one occasion when they were in the back seat snapping at each other. I felt embarrassed about getting angry with them, but I didn't always have the wherewithal to keep my temper.

I attended all their school open houses and teacher meetings, some of which were afternoon sessions. I was grateful that I could get away from work and make up time later. Billy's first- and second-grade teachers had noticed his withdrawing following Sue's death, and others, in later years, saw his blossoming and told me. He was a good student and a cooperative one. Anne matched Billy's academic achievements, helped her teachers during classroom activities, and made friends easily. For three years, she benefited from participating in a gifted and talented program, in which she received special attention one day a week to enhance her reading, writing, and artistic skills. Mrs. Knox, her teacher, spoke warmly and enthusiastically to me about Anne and her performance. I appreciated her special relationship with my daughter.

Overall the kids' teachers in our neighborhood public schools were skillful and committed, indispensable partners in helping them develop their educational and personal skills in childhood. They were also role models and caregivers who provided some of the emotional support the kids missed because of their mother's death.

After Sue died, Billy and Anne's grandparents had helped me move through a crisis period. As the kids grew older, they maintained and strengthened their relationships with us. We continued making visits to our cabin on Mekenok Island—trips that remained important for the kids and me, often because of the roles Ad played. He was an available grandpa to his grandchildren, especially to his grandsons. During each cabin visit, he took Billy and Brett, the son of Ad's son Bart, fishing together in many spots on the lake. He shared stories of his work with Native American tribes in the plains states and the experiences he'd had on the island. The kids, and sometimes we adults, listened to his stories and were nourished by his thoughts and insights.

Bart and I shared responsibility for the cabin upkeep. We repaired the pump that forced water from the lake through hoses to the cabin for washing and cooking. We built a two-story wooden stand for a large barrel that held the water. We reroofed the cabin with shingles to cover holes and give protection from bats and other critters.

In these and other maintenance jobs, Ad played knowledgeable supervisor. His message was that I was one of the family. Long before the needs of blended families were widely recognized, Ad set an example of attention and inclusion that I valued.

Irene engaged the kids in card and board games, preparing meals, and doing cleanup tasks. "We've got to sweep and mop this place before we use it," she'd say. She encouraged them to write letters to friends and other family members, and she read stories to them.

Sometimes she asked them to help her prepare food for the annual Fourth of July picnic. One year, she and Anne baked a large apple pie, which Anne carried the length of the island to bring for the meal. As she approached the table upon which to set the pie, she tripped on a large tree root. The pie flipped up in the air and fell on the ground, breaking into pieces. Anne looked horrified, began crying, and ran back to our cabin. I followed her. In the kitchen. she said, "Daddy, I made a big mess. I don't want to go back."

I said, "Folks like you a lot. And they know you had an accident, like everybody does. How about if we bring something else? Maybe some of those good Hydrox cookies?"

"Okay," she said. "But will you stay with me?" She took the cookies, and we walked back hand in hand. When we arrived back at the picnic site, Irene smiled and hugged her, the first of many folks who comforted her that day.

At home in Minneapolis, Irene and Ad did childcare, recognized all the important events in the kids' lives, and introduced them to stimulating cultural and entertainment experiences. An annual Christmas visit to the *Nutcracker* ballet started when Billy was small and became a family tradition. Irene helped me buy clothes, get haircuts, and drive the kids to their activities. She and Ad created a trusting, loving environment for both Billy and Anne. It was an immeasurable blessing.

On a personal level, Ad and I were friendly to and respectful of each other. There was some distance between us, but no competition or issues. He supported the parenting I did with the kids. Over the years, Irene and I developed what felt close to a mother and son relationship. She complimented me on my parenting and took an interest in my professional work. We had deep conversations about shared interests and concerns. It was wonderful to have a mother-in-law who was a friend, almost a best friend. How could I get luckier? My mom was certainly an important person in my adult life, but Irene's and my relationship ran deeper. She had lost the daughter whom I loved and married. That connection set our relationship apart from others and drew us together over her long life.

Grandpa Bob, too, remained part of our family for decades after Sue died. He lived in Leisure World, a retirement community in Seal Beach, California. When we visited him, he showed us the sights: Disneyland, Knott's Berry Farm, Universal Studios, SeaWorld, the *Queen Mary*, and his favorite restaurants. Bob taught Billy and me how to bodysurf on ocean waves at Seal Beach and Long Beach. When Anne was old enough, we helped her learn, too.

Bob and Billy had a special bond: they were athletic, easygoing, and consistent letter writers when not in each other's company. Billy told Bob about playing sports, his times with his friends, his school courses and grades, and his hobbies. He thanked him for his Christmas gifts and birthday money, which Bob sent regularly, and asked him about his jobs at Leisure World, his travels, and his favorite professional football team, the Los Angeles Rams.

One letter went deeper: "That was a very nice letter you wrote me. I will try and keep it for a long time. Easter is coming up and I'll be thinking of Mom a lot more, maybe you will be, too. It will be six years since she died and I miss her a lot. I hope Dad finds someone to marry before long. I think of her a lot in bed and in school. Maybe you do, too, but I still wish she was alive."

Billy and Anne were Bob's lifeline to Sue. He spent part of every summer with them and me, as he had with her. If we didn't visit him in Seal Beach, we did so in Ocean Park, Maine, and both were places of deep connection for all four of us. Years later, Billy told me, "The trips to see Grandpa Bob were priceless. The happiest times of my life were at the beach and with the people who had known and loved Mom. Ocean Park was magical. It elevated me."

I loved the fact that Bob engaged with the kids. He related to them in a spontaneous way and easily won their affection with his caring behavior and sense of fun. I asked him once, if he died and came back as an animal, what would he like to be? He said, "Oh, that's easy—an otter. I'd swim around and have a good time all day." He carried this attitude despite losing his only child and experiencing two divorces—one from Irene, which occurred after they had been separated during most of World War II, and a second from a woman who spent much of her life in a mental institution. None of those losses dimmed his generous spirit.

Bob and I had long talks about issues in education—we'd both been K–12 teachers—and about politics, world history, sports, entertainment, and many other things. He told me how much he respected my parenting and how glad he was that I continued to bring Anne and Billy, who were his only grandchildren, to him. We found it easy to talk to one another and to share common activities with the kids. Cooperation rather than competition between us was the rule. Bob was a father-in-law who treated me like a welcomed son: for the entire time I knew him, he gave me his regard and support, for which I was always grateful.

My mom was also a constant in the lives of Billy and Anne. For six years, she was a Friday regular at our house, taking care of them until Anne was ready for first grade and the need for her visits ended. Mom took this change in stride, knowing that the kids and I would still see her. She attended more art history classes—her favorites—saw her friends more often, and made sure, as did we, that she was involved in the signature events in Billy and Anne's lives.

Later I wrote a letter to my mom, as I had to my dad. I wanted to thank her for what she had done for me while she was still alive. In part, my letter read:

When I was a little child, you created a safe harbor for me—a calm place where food was good, sheets were clean, rooms were warm and tidy, my clothes folded and knitted just right, my toys were available, my friends were welcome, and I could always count on a bedtime story, usually snuggled close to you. It was a place, too, where I never heard cursing or saw violence—a gentle and peaceful place. When I was hurt in any way or scared, you were there to get me help or meet my needs. Because I lived in this kind of place, I know it helped me be a happy child.

In many ways, you made Grandpa's house our home. It seemed like every Sunday my aunts and uncles and cousins came to visit, and Jim and I played hosts to the little ones—sometimes two or three, sometimes five, sometimes 10 or more—with ghost stories, games, and sports. What fun that was, what a gift to have gotten to know my cousins, my extended family—and you were the one who made that possible.

I learned from you all through my childhood that home was a place in which I could trust, a welcoming place to which I could return. You did that, no one else.

I especially want to thank you for taking care of me during my childhood when things were hardest for you—when you had almost no money, when Dad disappeared, when you had little financial support from your own family, and when you had to get your first full-time job out of the home at age 40 to keep us afloat. It must have been very scary and very hard to have been the only single parent in a Catholic neighborhood at a time when no one was divorced and not one mother worked out of the home. I admire you, Mom, for your courage and I thank you for it.

After Sue died, thank you for coming every Friday all those years to care for the kids while I worked, and for staying over on the weekends so that I could have some free time and go out again. It was very hard for me, as a widower, to have had a five-year-old and a 10-week-old baby, and to have lost Sue. But I had a model to live by, someone who showed me that a single parent can work, can care for children, can be part of a large family, and can be alive and even well—that was you, Mom, and what I learned about determination, commitment, responsibility, and caring, I learned from you.

Now, at 85, you are still teaching me about life. I see how osteoporosis is bending your back, how lupus is slowing your walk, how scleroderma is hardening your fingers—these three diseases, ever punishing, always limiting you. But I want to thank you once more for showing me how to live each day—in making your meals, in talking with neighbors, in reading the paper, in writing notes to your grandchildren, in staying interested in and arguing politics, and more. You gave me life and you showed me, in so many ways, how to live it. I thank you for that and I promise to carry out your example.

I mailed the letter to Mom. When I didn't hear back from her about it, I asked her whether she had received it and what she thought of it. She said, "Yes, I got it. It was nice," then began talking about the upcoming Vikings/Packers football game. I was disappointed that she didn't tell me how she felt about the letter. But talking about her feelings was a rare thing for her to do, so I let the moment pass.

In 1981, I learned of a job opportunity at the University of Louisville. I had been at my University of Minnesota job for more than ten years by that point and thought I was ready to do the job my boss held, which wasn't going to be open anytime soon. The Louisville job looked like a carbon copy of his. I applied, was interviewed by phone, and was selected as one of five finalists. The university flew me to its campus for two days of face-to-face interviews and covered my expenses. I was excited. It was a thrill to be courted.

The interview with the search committee seemed to go well, as did interviews with budget-office and university professional staff. We talked with enthusiasm about the job duties, the culture of the office, and the benefits of living in Louisville—affordable housing, good schools, and an appealing climate. At a social event, people offered to show me houses, find nannies and daycare help, learn about the schools. I felt welcomed and respected. Folks were especially solicitous about my being a single parent—a single father—and offered support in practical ways. One said, "We're sure glad you applied and hope you get the job. This is a friendly place. We can settle you in a hurry."

With Billy and Anne being older, I thought it might be possible to leave Minneapolis and our family for what sounded like a good change. Still, if I got a job offer, I'd have to look very carefully at the impact of moving the kids. The risks were there, but so were the benefits: challenging work in a new setting, an increase in job responsibilities, a salary bump, and an opportunity to supervise others.

My last interview was with the university president, who would make the final decision. It didn't go well. He didn't seem to know much about the job, and he didn't seem interested in what I had done at Minnesota or what I might bring to the job. I asked more questions than he did. On the plane home, I thought I wasn't going to be offered the job. Sure enough, about three weeks later, I received a letter indicating another candidate had been hired. I was disappointed for a while but was still glad for the opportunity.

When the chance to teach graduate courses and do consulting projects in my field later emerged locally, I found I liked the mix of these activities, which also increased my income. I stopped looking for new out-of-state positions and focused on my life in Minneapolis.

CHAPTER 18

The Stages of Grief

✳ ✳ ✳

Amid the flow of family and school activities for both children, constructive as they were, ran another deeper reality that they and I experienced but rarely talked about: how we were each dealing with the grief of Sue's death. I knew about the famous "five stages" model of grief, proposed by Elisabeth Kübler-Ross in her book *On Death and Dying*, which was published well before Sue's death. The model was based on the author's interview research with patients who were dying. The five stages are:

Denial and isolation: "This can't be."
Anger: "It's not fair."
Bargaining: "I want them back."
Depression: "I miss them."
Acceptance: "I'm doing okay."

Kübler-Ross believed that most people go through these stages of grief, although not necessarily all of them or in the same order. I thought I had briefly moved through the five stages in the first year after Sue's death, from my disbelief at the time the paramedics were trying to revive her to my anger later that day, to many experiences wishing she was with us and missing her, to some kind of acceptance by the time I met and fell in love with Liz.

After the first year, my grieving—my really painful, tearful moments—lessened. What came next was sadness, loneliness, a sense of aloneness, still significant but not exhaustive in impact. Sometimes, looking at either Billy or Anne, I'd see a likeness of their mother in their features, how they moved, or how they talked. A glance at Sue's picture on a wall or in an album brought her back.

The house we lived in showed her aesthetic touch. I remembered buying a piece of furniture or a place setting or a coffee maker with her. She was everywhere, easily remembered. I knew that the kids and I would be linked throughout our lives by our shared experiences with her. Her loss ran too deep to be fully erased.

How I handled my feelings and memories of Sue fit a pattern described in *The Truth about Grief: The Myth of Its Five Stages and the New Science of Loss*, which a friend had given me. The book's author, Ruth Davis Konigsberg, said that Kübler-Ross's model of grief was not wholly accurate because she had based her research on a limited sample—only those who were dying. For her own research, Konigsberg interviewed people who were dying as well as their family members and friends, many of whom were their caretakers. She reached an additional conclusion about grief: she found that while the five stages might occur, most interviewees said that their strongest feeling was of overcoming loss, not merely accepting it.

I thought that I had accepted Sue's death and was in the process of overcoming it by functioning every day as a single parent as well as I could. To me, overcoming meant not letting her death create obstacles to what I thought I should be doing in work and family life. But I also set aside time to remember her and feel whatever feelings about her that emerged. I walked to a lake near our home or to parks or other quiet places to reflect on the relationship we had shared. Being in nature calmed me and prompted me to think of our time together, usually but not always our best moments. I remembered what Sue herself, a therapist, had told me: "Feelings aren't good or bad; they just are." It was a reminder to let my mix of feelings arise, experience them, and then move on. A simple notion, but not one I had understood growing up or as a young adult.

While I thought I had significantly worked through the stages of grief, coping with ongoing feelings of sadness, I didn't know where Billy and Anne were on their journeys. I watched for signs of how their mom's death might be affecting their attitudes or behaviors and asked Eldora and their grandparents to do the same.

None of us saw symptoms of trauma, like sleep disturbances, eating problems, or obvious anxieties. It was only much later, as adults, that they told me what they had felt as children about their mother's death. Billy said losing his mother was "a crater I continue to crawl out of, a weight, an overarching feeling, a constant pressure that would never go away, a space where there should be an important person that was empty." He felt this sadness through his school years and after, although he didn't talk much about his feelings with me or other family members.

Anne told me that even though she felt confident as a small child, she covered up her feelings of sadness. After many activities, such as sleepovers or school events, she was asked, "Is your mom picking you up?" Her answer—that she didn't have a mom, that her mom had died, and that her dad was coming—was greeted with silence. Few adults knew what to say.

Looking back to that time, Anne told me, "I always felt I was different. I was the only one without a mother, whether with friends, in our family—even in groups for survivors without mothers, I was the only one who had lost a mother at two and a half months. I missed her, cried myself to sleep many nights, but didn't show my feelings to others. I told people I was okay: 'I have a dad who is both a mom and a dad.' I was confident and happy, but sad. I held both kinds of feelings at the same time."

Anne learned to cover her sad feelings because, if expressed, they seemed to make others uncomfortable. Her consistently positive relationships and experiences with Eldora, her grandparents, other adults, her friends, and me helped compensate for losing Sue, she said. Underneath, however, her sadness remained.

In our present era, people often talk more openly about their grief and find ways to deal constructively with it. One of Anne's best friends and her husband honored the arrival and passing of their daughter, who was a few days old, by kayaking across one of our city lakes, where they scattered their baby's ashes. Afterward they had a party and prayed for her. They and their family and friends recognized their loss in ways that were meaningful to them and their circle of friends.

I realize now, with the benefit of hindsight, that I could have done more to help Billy and Anne recognize their loss. One approach I considered but didn't act on was family counseling. At that time, I thought that its purpose was to get help to manage problems or conflicts, not to enhance already successful relationships. Both kids seemed well adjusted, responsible, and happy, and I didn't think of using counseling to gain insight into how they felt on a deeper level.

Sometimes I attempted to have conversations with the kids about how they felt about Sue's death. Once, on Sue's birthday, I made dinner for all of us and asked them, "Have you been thinking about your mom's death? Would you like to talk about her?"

Billy responded, "It's okay, Dad. We don't need to do it now. There's something on TV I'd like to watch. Can I do that?"

Anne said, "Me, too." I let the moment pass. Someone with more skill might have found a useful way to broaden these questions into a conversation.

It didn't occur to me, either, that the kids might have trouble recognizing their own feelings. The whirlwind of everyday activities kept the three of us busy and worked against finding quiet times for similar conversations. Timing was important, too. It seemed to me that Billy and Anne were likely to be open to conversations about deep feelings only at particular times, not routinely. In that sense, they were like most adults I knew or had grown up with—and like me. Now I wish that I had found effective ways, whether through family counseling, conversations, or other approaches, to help them better understand the emotional impact of Sue's death on them. Later, as adults, through self-reflection, conversations with friends, or professional counseling, both made progress in recognizing and coping with their feelings of loss.

CHAPTER 19

Margaret

✳ ✳ ✳

As Billy and Anne got older, I thought we should look for a church for the three of us. I hoped that participation in a faith community could help us explore religious ideas and practices while connecting us with other families with whom we might build friendships. The Unitarian Universalist faith, which I believed promoted spiritual growth and social justice activities, seemed like a good fit for us. I had heard about it from Sue while she was still alive, from Irene, and from Bart and Cindy. I went church shopping.

The first church we tried had an inadequate children's program and an uninspiring worship service. We went twice before deciding to move on. The second was the UU church in our neighborhood at which we had had Sue's memorial service. I liked and admired its senior pastor, who had helped Ad, Irene, and me plan the memorial service.

On Easter Sunday, the sixth anniversary of Sue's death, the kids and I went to services. Billy and Anne attended the church's Sunday school, whose teacher they both liked. I found the adult service and the pastor's sermon affecting. Both melded together humanistic and Christian values in a powerful, persuasive fashion. Afterward, we three toured the church's library in search of new books to borrow. It was there that I met Margaret.

I turned from shelving a book, and we noticed each other at the same time. We both smiled, ever so slightly. Margaret was seated, holding the hand of a young boy, who looked about Anne's age. She had long brown hair, which flowed over her collar, and a sensitive and beautiful face. I had enough sense to walk toward her and begin a conversation. I didn't see a wedding band on her finger. We talked about our experiences in Unitarian churches and a little about single parenting before Billy and Anne joined us. I thought Margaret was smart, funny, warm, and attractive. I asked her for her phone number.

Margaret was divorced, and her son, Jack, was four. Throughout that spring and summer, she and I, and often our three children, shared picnics, walks, bike rides, movies, and meals. We lived on either side of Lake Harriet, ten minutes apart, which made it irresistible, it seemed, to connect for planned and spontaneous activities.

Remembering my experience with Liz five years earlier, I vowed to take my time building a romantic relationship with Margaret. The more I saw her, however, the less I kept the vow.

During the summer, we expanded our shared activities, with a trip to Mekenok with Ad, weekend trips around the state, and sleepovers, at first without the children and later with them. We five were comfortable and had fun with one another at the city lakes and our homes. Coparenting came easily to both Margaret and me. One night I watched as she brushed Anne's hair, with Anne on her lap; they were smiling as they talked quietly to each other. I loved that scene.

My birthday became an extended event. Margaret brought a lunch, with champagne, to campus, and we picnicked on the large, grassy mall in bright sunshine. A surprise dinner that evening featured balloons, streamers, favors, top hats, photos displayed from earlier months together, pictures drawn by our three kids, and a photo montage of us for my office. Her homemade Italian dinner was delicious, as was her homemade ice cream, for which she had recruited help from all three kids.

Over succeeding months, I became more and more attracted to Margaret. She had so many qualities I liked: intelligence, sensitivity, beauty, creativity, a sense of humor, warmth, and an affectionate nature. I thought she made responsible decisions about money and work issues and seemed committed to stepparenting and family life.

As we grew closer, we gained enough confidence to try a risky experiment: we did a five-minute sharing session in which each of us described a few limitations we perceived in the other. I said she tended to withdraw if we experienced conflicts, showed too much sensitivity to criticism, and seemed resistant to change, even in small matters. She told me, "You make judgments, could listen better, and don't give me enough distance when I need it."

It wasn't easy for either of us to hear these criticisms, but we thought it was a sign of our maturity—and the strength of our relationship—that we could. Neither of us had even thought of doing this kind of exercise before our first marriages.

On balance, we believed the positives we brought to our relationship and those with our children far outweighed the negatives. We fell in love with each other, foibles intact. By the end of summer, she suggested that she and Jack move in with me and my kids. "Jack and I are tired of living out of our suitcases. I love you, and I don't need to know anything more about you," she said.

I was ready and thought Billy and Anne were, too. I didn't give much thought to the possibility that things would not work out. I was sure living together would help us understand the needs and dynamics of blended family life. It could better prepare us for marriage if we chose it. I was lonely, too, and wanted Margaret's love and her nurturing of my kids. Bringing us together trumped continuing to date and living separately.

We combined households in my home, which also introduced Margaret and Jack to our next-door neighbor family. Their son, Mike, became Jack's best friend, mom Cindy his godmother, and Cindy and Margaret close friends. Ben—Jack's dad and Margaret's ex-husband—continued to be involved in Jack's life. When he came for Jack, he was gracious and friendly, which I appreciated. He didn't bring any conflict into our lives. Margaret and I began our blended family experiment with confidence.

In early fall, I thought we were succeeding in our everyday activities. All the kids liked their schools and were doing well in them. I continued my job at the university with an adequate salary and fringe benefit package to cover our needs. Margaret, trained as a teacher, opted at this time to be a stay-at-home mom, managing our home lives with thoughtfulness and care.

We bought new bikes for the kids, held a huge rummage sale, attended Billy's park league football games, and celebrated Halloween together.

Margaret and I collaborated on choosing after-school activities for the kids—not a small matter. We agreed on the amounts and priorities of the family budget. We identified three categories: yours, mine, and ours. Rent from her house went to her, my retirement dollars stayed with me, and we spread my salary between the two of us in recognition of my working out of the home and her working in it. We shared a commitment to involving our extended families in our activities, wanting all grandparents to have access to the kids.

We read a newspaper article that listed the "Ten Indicators of a Successful Relationship," starting with "handling finances," and we had them all. I thought we were acting like a pair of mature adults and stepparents—maybe even ahead of the curve. I was overjoyed to have found Margaret, someone who brought stability and a positive presence to our lives.

Before long, Margaret and I decided to get married. I had some initial reservations; I told her I thought we needed more time together, more distance from her divorce, more practice at being a blended family. I suggested we get premarital counseling. But she thought we were doing fine and didn't need counseling. "I think it's just going to get better," she said with a smile.

After thinking about it more, I lost my hesitation. It had been a relatively short time since we had met—eight months—but we both thought we and our children were ready. We could bring to our union the insights and practices from our earlier marriages and our experiences as single parents. We were both in our thirties. We thought we knew how to build and sustain a close relationship. After all, we had already been doing it.

The week before Thanksgiving, we married in our house, with a local Unitarian minister officiating. It was a smaller wedding than either of our first ones, attended by just a few of our family members and friends. Ad, Irene, and Mom were there, along with Margaret's parents. Bob came from California to give his support. Margaret's and my siblings were there, too.

We spent the long Thanksgiving weekend with Margaret's family at their Iowa home. We hiked over their forested and open land, crawled over tree limbs and log piles, shared good meals, and talked about work, politics, and our futures. I felt a sense of relief and gratitude.

We used a photo of Margaret, our kids, and me for our Christmas card that year. In the photo, we're all smiling.

CHAPTER 20

Surprises

✳ ✳ ✳

Two weeks after Thanksgiving, I came home from work and walked into our kitchen, where Margaret was standing. She didn't look happy. She said, "I've made a terrible mistake. I don't want to be married to you, and I don't want to be a stepmother. I don't love you. I feel trapped here, and I want to get out."

I was stunned. "I don't understand," I said. "We just got married!"

"I know that, but it was a mistake. I shouldn't have done it. And with Christmas soon, there's all kinds of family activities that I don't want to deal with. Things are only going to get worse."

Nothing in our relationship had prepared me for her pronouncement. I couldn't make sense of what she was saying, and the forcefulness and coldness with which she spoke frightened me. I felt awful, confused. We stared at each other for a while before I said, "Let's talk about this and what we're going to do." That evening began a long period of frustration and unhappiness for Margaret, me, and our children.

Christmas came and went, as did Jack's birthday and our previously planned February honeymoon in San Diego, California, with little joy for Margaret or me. Our honeymoon trip to the Hotel del Coronado, famous for its gracious style and lovely beach views, felt to me like a useless exercise. Pictures of us with family and acquaintances showed the truth: our inexpressive faces revealed how unhappy we were.

Before our trip, we met with Shirley, a marriage counselor recommended by a friend. Margaret wanted to end the marriage but agreed that we owed it to each other and our children to explore our feelings and options. We identified our expectations, all of which were in conflict: I asked for a commitment to the marriage; Margaret said she didn't trust or love me enough to give it. I asked for respectful, caring behavior from her; she said she often felt hostile, angry, and indifferent toward me. I wanted us to interact with all three kids more often and treat each one in a friendly way; she said she was feeling alienated when the five of us were together, trapped in stepparenting dynamics, her independence compromised. I asked for physical affection and lovemaking; she said she wanted distance and privacy. I asked for regular conversations about our life activities; she said I never stopped talking.

Our differences were enormous and our counseling agenda huge, almost too much to address. I felt discouraged, frustrated, unsure about our chances. She wasn't optimistic, either. But over the next several months, as winter ended and spring began, we tried.

Shirley helped, chiefly by giving us insights into our everyday behaviors and by suggesting ways to deal with our conflicting expectations. We didn't make any deep dives into the family dynamics that had influenced our personality development or analyze patterns we might be carrying forward from our previous marriages. We had to prioritize short-term crisis interventions for our failing relationship—what would help us to have, in Shirley's words, "livable days."

The to-do list was long. For Margaret, verbalize her feelings rather than shut down and distance herself. Initiate conversations with me and the children. Compliment me on things I did effectively for her and the children. Withhold sarcasm. Connect with us, especially with Anne, from whom she felt a lot of distance. For me, talk less; respond to her feelings more; listen carefully. Forgo analysis and introspection of her and our behaviors—be more accepting and less analytical. Ask her for physical intimacy. Make time with friends and family outside of the home; seek their companionship to partly meet my emotional and social needs. It was a complicated agenda for both of us.

We made some progress but still continued to separate from each other. We avoided conflict rather than deal with it. On one or two weekends each month, Margaret and Jack went to Iowa to be with her family. We often argued about those trips. I'd say, "Oh, you are going to Iowa again.

Terrific. What a great way to resolve our problems." She'd reply, "Better there than here." Neither of us was especially respectful to the other.

Margaret and Jack spent time with Ben, Margaret's ex-husband, for holidays or family milestones, sometimes in addition to my family but often in place of sharing time with us. I started teaching evening classes at the university and expanded a consulting practice. My teaching and consulting jobs took me out of the house several evenings a week and sometimes on Saturdays. I was free from her as she was from me.

With changes in our schedule, we saw Shirley much less. Easy and frequent conversations mostly disappeared, as did physical touching. Our face-to-face conflicts lessened, but our commitment to our marriage weakened. Overall, ambivalence characterized our time together—some closeness, some fun, followed by arguments and distancing. We were in a rocky place. I was discouraged, with little hope for the future of our marriage.

It was at this time that very, very unusual experiences occurred in our home, ones we thought were supernatural. They were mysterious, unpredictable, and not something we understood or could explain. On two occasions, Billy, Anne, and Jack were listening to music on a tape player in our basement when the player stopped without anyone touching it. All three kids were frightened and ran up the stairs to tell Margaret, who was in the kitchen.

On another occasion, Jack was in the basement when the lights began going on and off by themselves. When Margaret heard him scream, she opened the basement door and saw the wall light switch moving up and down by itself. On several nights while I was out, Margaret was in our bedroom with the door shut when it opened by itself and she felt cold air throughout the room. She was frightened, sensing that something was in the hallway. Once when she had this experience, she said she heard Billy cry out from his room. The next day, he told me that he thought there were ghosts in the house. Later in life, he said that at times he had felt his mother's energy in the house. It wasn't a bad experience, but it was unsettling for him when he was young.

During a weekend visit, Margaret's sister Tammy was standing at one end of our second-floor hallway when she saw an apparition at the other end. The spirit was life-size, gray, moving—a woman with discernible features. Frightened, she called to Margaret, who was in an adjoining room. When Margaret came to the hallway, the apparition was gone. Tammy was certain that she had seen it. We were all unsettled by these incidents.

I had left the Catholic faith during college, but I remembered that the church had exorcisms—rituals for ridding spaces of unwanted spirits. Margaret and I went to a neighborhood Catholic church to consult a priest. He advised us to purchase and sprinkle holy water—water he had blessed—in our house to exorcise the spirits. Margaret sprinkled the water in the second-floor rooms and hallway.

On a later occasion, while I was at work, she went to the basement. She felt coldness there, heard a discernible hissing sound, and felt her body being wrenched. Terrified, she ran upstairs without doing the exorcism, which she never tried again. About this same time, Billy's neighborhood friend Aaron watered plants in our house once when we were gone. He told Billy that he felt a presence, which he thought was Sue.

In a counseling session with me, Shirley, too, said that the spirit was Sue, coming back to protect her small children. Shirley thought that Sue knew that things were not going well for them. At a local Reiki conference that Shirley and Margaret attended, Margaret met a medium and asked him for help.

A day later, the medium called Margaret and said he had communicated at night with Sue's spirit: "She said she was feeling guilty, believed she had to be punished, was in an agitated state. After a while, she said she was free and would not be punished." The medium said Sue felt better and would not follow Margaret out of the house if she left. After that conversation with the medium, there were no more unusual incidents.

Some of the events weren't that out of the ordinary by themselves—a tape player misplays, an attic door blows open. But too many things had happened that were inexplicable in scientific or even conventional terms. Margaret's, Tammy's, and our children's stories seemed credible to me, even though I never experienced anything like them. The explanation that Sue or other spirits had visited us was as believable as any other.

I was concerned about the children's fears and watched for any lingering effects the encounters might have on them. I was glad that Sue had seemingly come back, I believed, to intercede in the toxic climate that existed in our house.

The experiences were extraordinary. They piqued my imagination and, in a way, offered relief from the difficulties I was experiencing in my marriage. For me, more ghost visits would have been welcome.

CHAPTER 21

Stepparenting

✕ ✕ ✕

While Margaret's and my relationship was difficult—filled with conflicts—we agreed on the need to stepparent our three children as well as we could. We both wanted them to relate to each other and to us in positive ways, despite the breakdown in our relationship. During the winter months, we took parenting classes at the Adler Institute in Minneapolis. We learned about Alfred Adler's ideas and practices in psychotherapy and tried to apply them to our situation.

Adler believed that children will seek the attention of their parents, through either positive or negative behaviors, and that parents must learn to cope with those behaviors. They can do that, he said, in a number of ways: Develop house rules. Communicate expectations about those rules. Set limits on behaviors. Introduce consequences. These ideas were consistent with those of Rudolf Dreikurs, whose major publication, *Children: The Challenge*, Margaret and I had both read.

Before she and I married, coparenting seemed easy for us. Our children got along well with each other and with us. We all had fun together. Margaret and I enjoyed being with them. Among the five of us, there were very few conflicts. When we asked the children to do something, they usually did it without fussing.

After we got married, things changed. There were a lot of fights. Jack took Anne's food without asking, bullied and hit her, and laughed when he succeeded in provoking either her or Billy. Anne whined over incidental matters or refused to cooperate with Jack on house projects. Billy interfered with Jack and his friend Mike's play and withdrew when he could have helped his younger siblings resolve an issue.

On one occasion, Jack pushed me out of a room when I was leaving for work and spat at me. Both Anne and Billy made faces at Margaret and ignored her requests. At times, all three sought our attention—Margaret's or mine—with negative behaviors. Both Margaret and I were discouraged by what the kids did to each other and to us. The early confidence we both had had that we were competent stepparents began to erode, just as our belief that we were well-matched partners had.

While she and I were challenged by the kids' behaviors—managing three was more work than two or one—we understood that they were experiencing and reacting to significant changes in their lives. They each had less one-on-one time with their biological parent and were expected to share that parent with another adult, while also getting along with new siblings and sharing space and resources with all these people.

Jack faced the most changes: new parent, new siblings, new home, new neighborhood, and new school. I wasn't surprised when once, after I disciplined him, with his hands on his hips and anger in his voice, he said, "You're not my dad. I don't have to do what you say."

Shirley helped Margaret and me understand the dynamics of our blended family and gave us tips. She said the kids had an investment in the comfortable past and saw the stepparent as an intruder. The kids were testing us and trying to drive us apart. She wanted us to talk with them separately as well as together and acknowledge the obvious—perhaps in a family conference. Her thinking paralleled that of Adler and Dreikurs.

Margaret and I established what we thought were commonsense house rules for the children. Among them: hang up coats, put shoes in place, pick up possessions, straighten rooms, bring toys inside the house, do some chores, treat each other with patience, avoid violence and abuse, cooperate as needed. We set and explained limits on behaviors and enforced consequences: disruptive behavior, for example, was not allowed, and if it continued after a warning, we removed whichever kid was at fault. The same was true with hitting, kicking, fighting, and destroying property or possessions.

There were positive consequences for positive behaviors. If the kids did well individually or as a group, we rewarded them with what they prized or enjoyed. We tried to be consistent in how we applied Adlerian thinking, treating all the kids the same or as close to the same as possible.

I approached my stepparenting of Jack with the perspective that he was another son, one who deserved the best parenting I could give—the equivalent to what I tried to give to Billy and Anne. I didn't always hit that mark. Margaret perceived that I sometimes undercut our house rules by playing favorites and by doing things that the kids could do for or by themselves. I felt we weren't creating a united front in dealing with different behaviors among the children when she treated Anne and Billy with what I saw as coldness, unfriendliness, and distance. In one of our counseling sessions, I pointed out that they wouldn't want to cooperate with her if she continued to seem uncaring. We both agreed that we needed to do better.

In late spring, Margaret and I were still in conflict about our approaches to parenting. A friend told us that the Family Education Center, a unit affiliated with the Adler Institute, offered consulting advice on stepparenting. To improve our skills, we participated in a center workshop in which staff learned that we had a blended family. They asked us to serve as a "teaching family" in another of their workshops. In this role, we were to identify a problem in our family and have our children join us in describing how we were dealing with this problem.

Margaret and I accepted the invitation and brought Anne and Jack with us for the next workshop. The problem we focused on, which chiefly involved the two of them, was arguing and fighting at the dinner table. The arguments were about which child got enough attention, exercised power inappropriately, or was discouraged about something.

The center's facilitator asked Anne and Jack how we could improve things—what approaches were Margaret and I taking or should we take? In front of the participants, the kids gave similar answers: "You know, sometimes we fight at dinner. Parents should settle things. They should send the kid who's making the trouble to another room—that's what our parents do. That's okay. It's a pain to have to listen to your brother or sister make noise or be stupid."

After our comments and a few questions from the audience, the facilitator and audience members told us what they liked about our case: Margaret's and my openness in discussing our problem, our obvious concern for our kids, and our success in applying Adlerian principles in our family. "What do we have to teach you?" the facilitator asked. He meant his question as a compliment. They liked the way the kids spoke up. They asked us to come back again to share other stories with them.

When we left the building, Anne and Jack joked around with each other. They had done well in a public setting and were very sweet with each other. We were proud of them and glad that, as a foursome, we had made a modest contribution to the center's programming.

I had been Jack's in-home stepfather for nine months. That was enough time to gain insights into my attitudes about stepparenting—and about its challenges, too. I accepted some ideas easily: Spend the money I make from my job to meet the needs of all the kids. Consistently treat each child fairly; don't show favoritism to my biological children. Attempt to understand each kid's physical and emotional needs and respond as best I can. Give time and attention to all three equally—reading stories, engaging in play, hanging out.

I had more trouble accepting Jack's negative behaviors than Billy's and Anne's. That was hard—I would get irritated over what he did far more than when they did the same thing. I struggled to ensure Jack's negative behaviors incurred the same consequences as Billy's and Anne's, not more. His behaviors pushed my buttons more quickly than theirs. I realized I sometimes had different attitudes about the kids and behaved differently toward them. I had to catch myself and stay aware of my bias every day.

CHAPTER 22

Uncertain Closure

✂ ✂ ✂

During the following summer, Margaret and I continued therapy with Shirley. We had applied some of her earlier ideas about living together more respectfully as well as Adlerian practices for parenting the children. Shirley took us into new territory: we began to see the impact of old patterns from our families of origin and our previous marriages, many of which were still operating in our marriage.

Margaret kept dealing with feelings of rejection, both from her father across many years and recently from Ben. While she and her ex-husband had been soulmates in many ways, she had discovered that they had different needs for intimacy that couldn't be reconciled. She was angry at the two men who played the most meaningful roles in her life. Some of that anger was redirected at me.

I eventually acknowledged that I had feelings of abandonment, driven both by my dad's uneven commitment to our family and Sue's unexpected, traumatic death. My long-running attempts to reconcile differences or estrangements in relationships—attempts to get closer—weren't always appropriate with Margaret or fitting for the circumstance. She felt they undercut her needs for independence, privacy, and space. We tried to keep these old inclinations in view but often struggled to do so.

We continued to work at being responsible parents to the kids, attempting to keep our relationship as a couple—with its problems—separate from our relationships with our three children. We prompted them to be active outside, to play and have fun together. With them, we biked around the lakes, went to nearby beaches, and involved them in planning a new back porch for our house, which was completed in July. They helped us to erect a large wooden swing in the backyard. Occasionally, we attended Sunday services at the Unitarian Universalist church.

As a family, we decided to get our first pets: two cats. We thought that our kids would learn how to take responsibility for them and would grow closer to each other in their shared efforts. We all went to the Animal Humane Society and picked out a tabby, whom we named Teddy, and a black and white one, who became Sammy.

The kids were expected to feed and provide water for the cats, take care of their litter box, and play with them. They rotated the support jobs and treated the two cats with affection. Margaret and I thought we saw bonding among the kids over the pets that hadn't been there before and some sweetness in each child as well. Our decision to become a pet family paid off initially.

During that summer, Margaret and I took the kids on a trip to Trout Lake, Minnesota, to visit with her family. Though the kids had fun fishing and playing, it was a downer for me. Her parents seemed indifferent to me, at best, and when I made a mistake starting a boat motor or with some aspect of a project, I kept hearing how "Ben was handy." The implications were clear.

Except for the Trout Lake trip and one visit to Mekenok, the five of us began heading in different directions. Margaret and Jack made longer trips to Iowa by themselves as Billy, Anne, and I did to Mekenok. I sent Billy and Anne to visit Bob and our East Coast family members in Maine. Bob had high compliments for both, writing me, "They are models—so helpful, cooperative, unselfish with us and between each other. They don't complain. We all loved having them with us."

Bob found that neither child had much good to say about our home life in Minneapolis, their relationship with Margaret, or my parenting. He revealed that Billy told him, "Dad and Margaret play favorites—it's Jack. He gets away with all kinds of things. Once, when he kept interrupting me when I was on the phone, I asked him to stop ten times. When he kept it up, I kicked him. I didn't hit him hard, but Margaret came over and kind of tapped me in the stomach—'Hit for hit for bullying,' she said. She didn't do a thing about him." Anne said, "She won't read to me at night. She has never kissed or hugged me. When she combed my hair last year, that was one of the few times."

Neither Billy nor Anne was happy to talk with me on the phone during their trip, and they ended our conversation quickly. They told Bob they didn't care if I had called or not. I was discouraged by their attitudes, but I understood them. The change from a year earlier was unmistakable. I—and, to some extent, Margaret—had tried to connect with each kid in positive ways, to treat all of them equally, but it was clear we weren't routinely meeting all their expectations. Stepparenting, especially in an unhappy environment, was hard.

As summer ended, however, Margaret reached out to me in ways I hadn't expected. She said she was lonely and wanted to be close to me, physically and otherwise. She discontinued her weekend trips to Iowa. She suggested and arranged a fall vacation for us to Tofte, a picturesque small town in a forested area of northern Minnesota near Lake Superior. She agreed to return to counseling with Shirley "to explore possibilities." She began planning a new flower bed in our yard for the next spring. She was friendly and warm to me. Autumn became a time of renewal for us. "I want to try again," she said. I loved all of it.

Then, in early November, after a three-day weekend with her sister, she told me, "My feelings about you have changed. I don't feel good about you. I want to give notice to my renters by November 30 and go. It's the right thing for me to do."

I blew up. "God damn you. What kind of person are you? You said you'd work on our marriage with Shirley, and you haven't. How selfish. How could you do this to the kids and me?"

"I understand why you are angry."

"Angry? I'm not just angry. I'm hurt. You don't care about us. Just get out of this house. As soon as possible. I can hardly stand to be with you."

She didn't immediately give notice to her renters. Throughout the month, we talked about whether she would go or stay. In one conversation, she told me she distrusted all men except Ben and a number of gay men she knew.

"How could you marry me?" I asked her.

"I thought I was getting someone like Ben. But it was too soon since the divorce. And you and I have real differences—incompatibilities—that I didn't see."

I paused and then said, "I get that, but what if we use a three-month period, maybe December through February, to try one more time? To work on our differences? After that, we can decide if we stay together or separate."

"What about one month? I still love Ben. I like being with him—I want to get back together. Actually, I feel guilty about not proposing an open marriage with him. I'll work with Shirley about my feelings about him."

"I can't believe this. I feel used. This is ridiculous, awful—you made a commitment to me."

"I hadn't planned to make you miserable. I didn't know when we got married that I still loved Ben."

"I need a real wife. You are not it. You better go."

Later that night, she told me she'd talk to Shirley about her feelings about Ben and about staying. By the end of the month, she had made her decision. She would leave by the first of January. She told me she didn't love me enough to stay.

"There must be ten thousand women in Minneapolis who would like to be married to you. You are a generous, loving, warm, giving man. But I want to be independent."

We both cried and held hands. After she went to bed, I sat in the living room looking at the fireplace, too sad to move. I didn't want to go to our bedroom. Is there a worse feeling than lying next to someone you love who doesn't love you? I can't remember where I fell asleep that night.

When I told Anne that Margaret and Jack were leaving and didn't know if or when they might be coming back, she said, "It's okay with me if they come back, but Margaret's got to treat me nice." Billy said, "She was pretty nice to me. Not always, but a lot of the time. And I kind of liked having Jack as a little brother. But if they're gone for good, I am not even going to think about them. It'll be like they were never here." What I thought I heard from the kids was ambivalence—no great sadness or desire for reunion. Whatever happened would happen.

On December 31, Margaret and Jack moved out. Before the van arrived, she said, "I'm not sure about this. Maybe I should stay until February. Try again."

"Go, go, go. I can't stand this jerking back and forth. We can use the time apart for a break, get some space, sort things out more, and maybe start over. It's not working this way. It may, if we try another approach. You've got to go."

After they had gone, I realized Margaret and I were in role reversal from my experience with Sue. In my previous marriage, I was unsure about keeping a commitment and left her, though temporarily. In my marriage to Margaret, she was the one who couldn't make a commitment and left. Sue and I had used our separation to rebuild our relationship and renew our life together. I wasn't sure that Margaret and I could duplicate that outcome. I had fallen in love with and married someone who appeared to have the maturity and skills—and had made the commitment—to be a lifelong partner in a blended family. I ended up living with someone who helped create the most miserable extended period of my adult life and did almost nothing to nurture my children.

Still, I wasn't ready to end our marriage. I was drawn to Margaret, not by the kind of love I once felt for her, but certainly by curiosity and a little hope. What had caused the dramatic flip in her attitude and feelings toward me? It was a mystery to me, although we had some insights into her history, her needs, and mine as well. Did she have the capacity to change? To be the way she had been before we married? Could she recommit to our marriage? What could I do better or differently that might enhance our relationship?

I wondered whether a separation might help turn things around for Margaret and me, as it had with Sue. I didn't know, but it seemed premature, despite all the bad moments, to stop trying. There were our children to consider, too. If we rebuilt the blended family, all three might benefit. They were only five, six, and twelve years old, young enough for us to craft positive, meaningful relationships with all of them.

CHAPTER 23

Moving On

❂ ❂ ❂

I began the new year in familiar territory: as a single father for Billy and Anne. Margaret and Jack were gone, but I continued established routines for the kids. They went to the same neighborhood schools and after-school activities, and they spent time at Mom's and Ad and Irene's homes.

Billy saw more of his neighborhood and school buddies, and Anne spent more time with Beth, her best friend, who lived across the street from us. She began piano lessons. "Beth's taking lessons, Daddy. Maybe we can play together if I get any good," she said. *Why not try?* I thought. I felt lucky that so many options were available.

Since the experiment with the kitties had gone well, we added another cat, named Mario. He replaced Sammy, who'd gone with Margaret and Jack. In a short time, we discovered that Mario was disabled—he couldn't jump from place to place without falling awkwardly, had trouble remembering where his food and litter box were, and seemed confused. Anne said, "Daddy, is Mario going to be okay or can we get help for him? He's not doing so good." After a few weeks of similar behavior, and being picked on by Teddy, we decided it was best to return Mario to his former owners. The family that had sold the litter of cats from which Mario had come took him back, with apologies. "They'll take care of him better than we could," Anne said.

The kids and I picked out another black and white kitty at the Animal Humane Society, whom we named Joey. He was a sweetie, a calm cat who would lie on our chests and put his paws around our necks. He and Teddy got along, since Teddy ignored him. The cats took turns sleeping at night on either of the kids' beds, with Teddy eventually settling in with Billy most nights and Joey with Anne or, at times, on his pillow in our kitchen.

After Billy and Anne showed me that they could care for the cats, we decided we were ready for a dog. We selected a sheltie, a smaller version of a collie. Shelties are affectionate, obedient, intelligent dogs, the research said, the kind we thought would be a good fit for us. I bought one, caramel and white, from a local breeder and surprised the kids with him before our supper. They whooped when they saw him and ran him around our backyard on a leash. That night we named him Max. He would live with us for sixteen years before he died, matching Teddy's equally long run with us.

In later years, we added fish and a hamster, which Anne cared for, a parakeet, which we eventually gave to my mom, and a pair of gorgeous lovebirds. These last had striking green, orange, and yellow markings, seemed well matched to each other, and were easy to care for. We kept them in a white cage, which we hung in the dining room by a large window, where they were warmed by regular sunlight. We all took turns in the feeding and cleanup of the birds. We could hear their cooing and the flutter of their wings when we were in other rooms on the same level of the house. It was fun to have all these critters around, even though caring for them at times had its downsides—for example when they were sick, made messes, or ran away.

One event with the pets left a lasting feeling of frustration and sadness for Anne and me. She and I had walked through our front door when we heard a racket inside the house—the birds were cawing, and there seemed to be an intense hissing sound in the air. We looked into the dining room and were startled to see Teddy hanging on to the birdcage.

Although the cage was at least four feet off the ground and not near the dining room curtains, he had jumped onto it and opened its door. He had one of the birds in his mouth and was shaking one of his paws at the other, who was fluttering wildly in the upper part of the cage. Teddy was snarling and the bird was shrieking loudly. Anne called out, "Oh Teddy, stop, stop, stop! Let go!" We both ran into the dining room, but I told Anne to stay back and put my arm in front of her to slow her down. I was afraid that, in his agitated state, Teddy might lunge at her and bite her.

Teddy turned his head, saw us coming, and jumped from the cage to the floor. I could see that the neck of the lovebird was broken, his little head hanging limply as Teddy clamped his mouth on his body. I reached for Teddy, but he broke away, running down to the basement, leaving a trail of green and red feathers. I told Anne to close the birdcage to keep the other bird inside, and then I followed Teddy, grabbed him by his neck, and pulled the bird's dead body out of his mouth.

We decided to bury the bird in a wooden matchbox in our backyard flower bed. Anne made a tiny marker and a cross out of Popsicle sticks for the grave site. "He never got to go outside before, Daddy," she said, looking sad, as she smoothed dirt over his little plot.

Although the pet store owner from whom we bought the lovebirds told us neither bird would live long if the other died, we decided to try our luck keeping the survivor. We loved his music and his beauty. We moved his cage to a place where Teddy could not mount another attack. The bird lived for years with us before we decided to return him to the pet shop so he could be reunited with another of his kind.

I thought our menagerie of pets was worth every cent we spent and every moment we shared with them. We gave them what they needed, and, in varying degrees, they returned attention, companionship, and affection to all three of us. They became valued members of a family that had experienced significant losses. Their presence comforted us. We three did well, too, in managing as many as we had. The kids would be prepared if they decided to be pet owners as adults.

With Margaret and Jack out of our house, I had more time for participating in family activities with Billy and Anne and more time for work, too. I expanded my consulting practice with school districts and universities while continuing my administrative job. I asked my boss at the university to go to a four-day work week, giving me a three-day weekend and better work/life balance. It was a win-win situation for both of us: I was in the office enough to do my job duties, and he realized savings enough in the budget from my reduced salary to use for other purposes. I was making enough consulting money to offset the loss of one day's pay and had flexibility I hadn't experienced before. My new schedule stayed in place for years until other opportunities emerged for me.

It was challenging, however, to do the consulting projects in combination with my day job while being a full-time single parent. As much as I could, I scheduled consulting activities on Fridays and Saturdays and occasional weekday evenings. These latter sessions were unavoidable, especially when I worked with school districts whose staff had little free time during workdays. It helped that Billy was now thirteen and Anne eight. He was old enough to responsibly babysit her at night, and if he wasn't available, I brought her to one of her friends' homes or to Ad and Irene's. At times I scrambled but was able to find good care.

On one college consulting job, I worked regularly in the city of Rochester, located about eighty miles from Minneapolis. Once, while I was there, it began to snow hard. The forecast predicted a blizzard. By 9:00 p.m., when I finished my work, local buildings, roads—everything was almost invisible from the falling snow. I telephoned the kids to say that it was too dangerous to drive back and that I would need to stay in a motel overnight.

I headed for one nearby but then changed my mind. I didn't feel comfortable staying away the whole night. I turned onto the freeway leading back to Minneapolis and followed directly behind a huge snowplow that was clearing the roadway. I could see only about ten feet ahead of me but managed to keep my car in its lane, despite strong winds and slippery pavement. The drive, which normally took less than an hour and a half, lasted almost three hours that night. I didn't see another car on the road.

When I got home, both Billy and Anne were still up, although it was a school night. They were relieved to see me.

"I had to come back, guys. I am sorry I didn't call. Once I got on the road, I couldn't."

"We wondered what you were going to do. You always come home," Billy said.

"I kind of thought you would come back, even though you said you were going to a motel. I was worried," Anne said.

"I didn't feel right. I wanted to be back with you two."

We hugged each other, smiled, and headed to bed. The trip had been risky, but staying away felt worse.

Sometimes I attended professional conferences out of town for several days, during which I often hired college students to watch the kids. One was devoted to vegetables for herself and for them. When I got home, Anne said, "Daddy, can we have different help when you are gone? Broccoli, broccoli, broccoli. Yuck. And she made us stay at the table until we finished it." Finding perfect help was hard to do, but I kept on looking.

CHAPTER 24

One More Try

❋ ❋ ❋

At the same time that my marriage was stuck in uncertainty, my work life was taking off. I was confident outside the home while being far less inside. I decided to go slowly in trying to improve my relationship with Margaret. In one of our first conversations after she moved out, I suggested that we try "dating" again, if and when either of us wanted that. I told her I thought more time with Shirley might also be helpful, together or separately, if we wanted. No proposed timelines. No pressure. The remaining winter months passed with little contact between us.

In late March, I went to a movie with an old friend, a woman with whom I did not have a romantic relationship. In the lobby of the theater, I ran into Margaret, who was with a male companion. Like young teenagers, we gaped at each other, began an awkward conversation, and shuffled away. I think we both assumed the other was on a date. The next morning, she called and invited me to come over on Friday night, a few days away. I went for what turned into a three-day weekend reunion of conversation and closeness.

It felt like a return to the start of our relationship exactly two years after the fact. Mutual attraction, easy companionship. Later in spring, I invited her to dinner at my house, which led to more of the same—a period of wine and roses, I thought. But in other conversations with her, I felt the coldness and indifference that had contributed to our separation. Neither of us proposed ending that separation, nor did we go to marriage counseling together.

I saw Shirley several times by myself, once prompted by rereading love letters that Margaret had written to me in the summer before we moved in together. Reading the letters, filled with warmth, respect, enthusiasm, and caring, left me raw emotionally. Shirley told me, "Margaret still cares for you, but I don't know that she wants to change. Don't get your hopes up. Keep your distance from her and take care of yourself. You don't have the energy to deal with her now. You might hold back on a divorce, too, until you are ready to take on that process."

In the summer months, Margaret and I had little contact with each other. Anne resumed horseback riding lessons, and Billy played baseball. The kids and I went to Mekenok, often bringing their friends or playing with other kids on the island. Sue's stepbrother and family and our friends the Israel family came to visit us there as well. In early August, we met Bob in Ocean Park. We had a reunion with our East Coast relatives—a nurturing experience. It was hard to leave.

That summer we also participated in a Wachtler family reunion, which brought members of Mom's family of origin to St. Paul. Mom had seven siblings, many of whom were still alive. They and their children lived in Minnesota, Illinois, Texas, Ohio, and elsewhere. They joined us on a brilliantly sunny day for conversation, games, and great outdoor food. The two reunions with our family members from all over the country gave the kids and me a huge boost.

Back home, Billy and Anne talked about what fun they had had with their cousins. These summer experiences contrasted with the rejections they had both experienced from Margaret during the previous year.

In August, Margaret called me to say she was ready to go back to counseling but didn't want to see Shirley, our regular therapist. "I don't trust her," she said. "Do you know someone else? I'm being pulled both ways. I want distance from you, but I want to be close to you. Counseling might help."

I arranged for an initial meeting with Roy, a Unitarian Universalist pastor who was also a licensed marriage counselor. It was a tense session at which both Margaret and I cried, but each of us thought it was worthwhile—without blame, we revisited issues about our differences. We planned a return session in a few weeks. The morning of that session, as agreed, I called her to confirm the time I would pick her up.

"I've been thinking a lot about it. I don't want to go to counseling again with you," she said. "I don't want a relationship with you. I don't want a divorce now, but if you do, go ahead."

I heard what she said and couldn't believe it, but I didn't try to talk her out of anything. I said, "Okay," and hung up.

I kept our scheduled counseling session with Roy by myself. I told him I felt whipsawed by this latest conversation with Margaret and from two years of ambivalent experiences with her. I was discouraged and wondered what to do.

He said he could see why I was drawn to her but that intimacy seemed to be a problem for her. He didn't think she was going to change. "You're like an alcoholic, going back for a quickie. You can stay, but don't expect much. And try not to think about the good times with her, either," he said. He encouraged me to work with an attorney if I decided to seek a divorce. When I was leaving, he asked, "Did you miss some of the signs? Are you picking the best women for you?"

I left Roy's office and walked past the snow that covered his lawn and spilled into the street. It was a cloudy, cold day in early November, almost two years to the day that Margaret and I had married.

I felt that Margaret's and my relationship was not going to improve and that things would not get better for Billy and Anne, either. Maybe I was wrong, but where was the evidence? I had spent a year trying to repair my marriage. I decided it couldn't be saved.

I met separately with two divorce attorneys, who outlined the legal requirements and issues in seeking a divorce. There was little difference in their description of divorce procedures. They thought it could be done simply and fairly and at little cost.

After those meetings, I weighed the options and, before Thanksgiving, decided to ask Margaret for a divorce. I wrote her a letter asking for an un-contested divorce and said I would call her to set up a meeting to discuss the issues that were important to us.

She agreed, and we met a couple of times before the year ended. In our first meeting, I asked her why she hadn't kept our appointment with Roy.

She said, "I was afraid I didn't love you enough. I got some counseling by myself and confirmed that."

"You took care of yourself at my expense. You hurt me terribly. Our plan was to rebuild our marriage. That's what I heard across the last couple of months. How could you do this?"

"I'm sorry. I know I hurt you."

We sat hand in hand. She smiled a little. I felt a warmth in her voice, a softness in her touch. She seemed like the woman I had first met, the one with whom I had fallen in love. So attractive and appealing. But Roy was right. I had to let go.

I petitioned Hennepin County Family Court and had her served with divorce papers. We met to discuss how to complete the stipulation document required for review by the court, which chiefly set out how we would resolve bills, share personal property, and meet any other financial obligations. We treated each other with courtesy and no rancor.

After we reached agreement on the document and I was about to go, she said, "I'm celibate now. A while ago, I got lonely for you and almost called you, but I held back." I looked at her and said nothing. It was almost too much to hear.

When I told the kids that Margaret and Jack would not be returning and that she and I were getting a divorce, neither had much reaction. Anne nodded and continued doing her homework assignment. Billy said, "She was nice to me, but I figured they weren't coming back." A year apart had created distance between the two of them and the three of us.

Billy later told me that he felt a sense of loss over our breakup, something I hadn't heard from Anne. As his stepmother, Margaret had sometimes given him attention and treated him with regard. He often felt close to Jack, too. He liked having a little brother. Before high school, he had now lost a mother whom he'd remembered, a stepmother, and a stepbrother—more losses than any other child I knew. At times he was angry and frustrated about his circumstances, understandably so. I wanted more for him and felt bad that I hadn't found a stepmother or partner who might have made a difference in his and Anne's lives.

In April, the month in which I had met Margaret three years earlier, I went to the courthouse in downtown Minneapolis. I felt the same way I had when I wrote her my letter asking for the divorce: relieved, sad, and unsure about what had happened in our relationship and what was ahead for the kids and me. I also felt like a failure. I fell in love with Margaret, decided to build a serious relationship with her, chose to marry her, lived in marriage with her, and ended our marriage and relationship. How could I have been so mistaken about her?

My attorney and I attended the courtroom hearing. By agreement, Margaret was not present. I felt numb. I stood still and listened. I was not asked any questions and did not speak. I was a bystander at my own divorce.

After the court proceedings, I drove south on the I-35W freeway, past apartment buildings in Minneapolis, car dealerships in the inner-ring suburbs, shopping malls in the further suburbs, open, undeveloped land beyond the suburbs—none of this trip planned. The sun shone through my car windows, and I could see the brown of the land beginning to green out with the coming of spring. I felt worse now than I had before I entered the courthouse. Tears came.

I ignored Roy's advice and thought almost exclusively of the good moments with Margaret and our three children—chiefly in the months before we married, when the signs seemed right. "I love you and I don't need to know anything more about you," she had said.

I kept driving until I realized that I needed to pick up Anne, whose after-school class would be over. I felt very tired and, at that moment, defeated.

CHAPTER 25

The Meditation Group

✼ ✼ ✼

During my separation from Margaret, I became an active member in a group of adults who were interested in exploring ideas about religion and spirituality. Rich, a close friend, had invited me to join the group, knowing that I was struggling with issues of faith and that I wanted to find a church home for the kids and me. He thought I'd benefit from discussions of religious faiths and practices, and I did.

What I didn't realize was how much I would learn from group members about parenting, stepparenting, and the challenges of managing family life. They, too, faced complicated issues, and they shared helpful insights with me about how they addressed them. In time, their regard and support for me as a friend gave me confidence to keep going as a single parent. For me, my participation was about more than investigating the mysteries of faith.

The group's members included a nurse, social worker, writer, public manager, planner, human services professional, physicist and nature photographer, marketing professional and nature photographer, educator, and homemaker—five couples and me. Most of us had been raised in the Christian faith, especially Catholicism, but had drifted away from it. We were looking for ways to understand religious and spiritual experience, which we didn't think were the same thing. To us, religious experience consisted of faith in an established religion, of one denomination or another, and commitment to its worship and outreach activities. It was about connecting to a church or other organized faith community.

Spiritual experience usually did not include belief in a particular religious faith and participation in its church activities, although it might. Spirituality dealt chiefly with exploring the mysteries of life: Is there a God? What's the nature of the universe? What's our life purpose on this earth? Is there life after death? How may we be good stewards of the time and resources we use? These kinds of questions and their answers were important to us and took us beyond exclusively humanistic perspectives.

My experiences with Sue's death and with what I thought were spirits in our home—including her specifically—also motivated me to learn more about mystery, about the connection and divide between existence in our material world and what lies beyond it. That interest was reinforced by Margaret's experience with the medium. How do we understand and explain the communications with spirits that mediums claim are real? I wasn't sure.

I was also thinking about how to chart a path to a religious faith and church for myself, Billy, and Anne, for which I didn't have immediate answers. During my marriage to Margaret, we had drifted away from the Unitarian Universalist experience. I wanted to explore further, with a trusting group, different ideas and practices about both religious and spiritual life. Better to do it with fellow travelers, I thought, than by myself.

We agreed on a monthly meeting agenda: do a meditation, discuss our reactions to it, have a meal or dessert, and share news of our work or families. We agreed to rotate meeting sites and responsibility for managing the meeting agenda and meals.

The first topic our group explored was meditation itself—what it was and how to do it. Some had previous practice; many of us did not. We drew ideas from many sources, especially from the writing of Jon Kabat-Zinn in his book *Wherever You Go, There You Are.* Kabat-Zinn writes that the purpose of meditation is to be mindful, to be open to the present moment. It is the opposite of letting ourselves run on automatic pilot, living our lives in repetitive, unreflective fashion. It is an approach for touching conscious and unconscious perspectives.

In our meditation practice, we sat up straight in our chairs, put our hands on the tops of our legs, closed our eyes, became silent, and concentrated on our breathing. Before and while we meditated for fifteen to twenty minutes, the host couple played soothing music, such as a recording of the ocean surf, a river running, quiet sounds from the forest, or Native American drum or lute music. We either used the guided imagery approach, in which the host described or read about an image or a picture upon which to focus, or individually concentrated on a vision of our own. Doing this exercise invariably involved letting go, stripping away thoughts and feelings about the past, as much as possible, and quieting ourselves. When we did it, and avoided falling asleep, our imagination took us places, some of which were dreamlike and almost all of which were new.

In our first meditation, I saw myself as an old, old man, stooped over, with a gray shawl draped over my shoulders, standing on my back porch. The porch faced our backyard, which had a lawn, two large trees, many bushes, a two-car garage with a basketball backboard and hoop, and a wide driveway. In my meditation, every inch of the lawn was filled with poppies, red, orange, and white, many of whose stems and petals swayed in a light breeze. The sky was blue, cloudless, and the sun shone brightly. Anne was a grown woman and stood next to me, her hand resting on my right shoulder. The sun was in my eyes, but I could make out a small smile on her face. I felt her warmth, her caring presence. Billy, standing next to the porch steps, was also grown. He was looking at Anne and me, his hands on his hips, and he smiled broadly. Behind him, several teenagers—my grandchildren, I thought—were shooting baskets in the driveway, surrounded by sunlight.

I felt incredibly happy, appreciative, and relieved. I was at peace. Tears started to form in my eyes. My children and I were adults together; we had made it. We were beyond the challenges of their childhoods, with new opportunities in work and life for all three of us. When I finished the meditation and explained what I had seen to the group, I felt I was describing a real past experience involving our family. It was wish fulfillment to be sure, like a memorable dream. Such power in a single meditation! I was hooked.

When we finished dessert at this first meeting, we shared stories about what was happening in our work and home lives. I hadn't anticipated how beneficial this part of each meeting would be. In almost all meetings that followed, members told stories of the challenges they were facing:

A middle school child addicted to drugs who had trashed the house. A child with heart problems unlikely to lead to full recovery. A difficult divorce. Tight family finances. For many, relationships with parents or siblings that had collapsed and seemed irreparable. I was not alone in my struggles as a single father. We talked with candor and honesty with one another as we sought answers, however short-term, to the problems we experienced—a huge gift for me and for others.

We ended our first meeting with an eleven-person circle hug, arms draped around each other's backs or shoulders, swaying a bit left and right. This became a signature act in all succeeding meetings. We said goodbye holding each other.

As I drove home, I felt freer, more at ease with myself and my world, more as one with my surroundings, physical and spiritual. The demands of my work and family life seemed more manageable. I was optimistic. When I got home, I checked Billy's and Anne's bedrooms. He was in bed reading a book, with his headphones on, in his world. She was asleep in her bed, a book she had read on her end table. I felt such joy that they were my children, safe, healthy, and with me.

In our monthly meetings, we explored a number of fascinating subjects, the most important of which for me was the mind/body/spirit paradigm. Drawn from Confucian, Hindu, and Buddhist religious beliefs, its major assumptions are that each human being consists of fields of energy—physical, emotional, mental—that flow through seven centers in our bodies, called chakras, affecting all cells of our body. Illness occurs when these energies are misaligned and out of balance. The tools of Eastern medicine—meditation, acupuncture, massage, nutrition choices, yoga, tai chi, and others—help us restore the energy balances and improve our physical, emotional, and mental health. They can contribute to our spiritual well-being as well. Until I joined the group, I hadn't known about this integrated model or its potential for powerfully and positively impacting our lives.

After each discussion, I reinforced some mind and body activities I had been doing with Billy and Anne and added new ones. We made more trips to our local public libraries and asked more often for books as gifts from our relatives and friends. I intended to read more to Anne before bedtime, but when I sat on her bed one night, she said, "It's okay, Daddy. I can read to myself now." I was surprised but didn't push back. She had taken on the job herself.

I talked more with the kids about their school activities and homework, about what they were interested in and learning and how I could help them. We used our YWCA membership more often and increased our outside exercising and playing, almost regardless of the weather—more tobogganing, snowball fights, walks, bike rides, ball playing. Expanding physical activity was a plus. I looked more carefully at what we were eating, buying foods with higher nutritional value. We shopped occasionally at co-op grocery stores, which were becoming more popular at that time. We cut back on our trips to McDonald's; chicken and broccoli began to replace red meat.

While I wasn't ready to go back to a church with the kids, I talked with them about spiritual topics we had addressed in our meditation group meetings. One was about the near-death experience (NDE), a heavily documented phenomenon throughout the world. NDE participants were uniformly in crisis situations, often in surgery, when they had an out-of-body experience: they saw their bodies on the surgeon's table from above, passed through a powerful tunnel of white light into a fearless environment, felt the most happy and gratified of any time in their lives, and then, faced with a decision to remain in this circumstance or return to their bodies, chose to return. Most concluded that their deaths would involve experiences similar to NDE.

I described NDE to Billy but not to Anne. I thought he would understand the explanation without being frightened by its prospect, but it seemed to me too complex a topic to discuss with Anne at age nine. I told Billy that, in the Bible and in other religious stories, the same kind of white light described in NDE experiences was attributed to Jesus and spiritual beings.

"When Mom died, I hope she had this white light thing. Maybe that's what it is like wherever she is, and she feels okay," Billy said.

"Me, too," I said. We didn't have an explanation for the possible existence of the white light but found it a reassuring idea, especially when we thought of Sue.

In addition to talking about religious and spiritual subjects in our group meetings, we addressed issues related to marriage and family relationships. All of us were or had been married. All of us parented our children or other young family members. We hoped to learn more about being better partners, parents, and relatives. We often talked about how to deal with change in ourselves, our loved ones, and our relationships.

Out of our discussions came a powerful insight that helped me better understand my relationships with Sue and Margaret and with others in my family and in work settings: you can change yourself, but you can't change others. All of the talking I did, the feelings I showed, and how I behaved wouldn't change others. People will change only when they want or need to. They might change in response to something I've done, but I couldn't make them do it—forcing them might work temporarily, but it wouldn't last for very long. This insight sounds simple, but it was very difficult to incorporate into my relationships. I wasn't used to thinking that way.

For decades, I'd carried certain attitudes, such as "I am a pretty smart guy." "I have the right answers to almost all questions." "My ways of doing things are better than those of others." I was irritated when others didn't do what I expected of them—*What's wrong with them?* I thought. No problem with self-confidence for me!

Once I understood that I couldn't automatically or permanently change other people, I wanted to learn more: How did I really interact with other people? Was I respectful to them? What values and beliefs were at my core? What should I change in myself? My new expectation was that people around me may or may not change, but I needed to be a responsible, less critical, more humble person. These insights complemented what I had learned in counseling about how to be a better husband and friend in romantic relationships, especially the notion of "listen more, control less."

In my time with the group, I didn't find a religious faith or church denomination for the kids and me. I still wasn't sure what I believed, and I couldn't fake a commitment when it wasn't there. But I learned that others were struggling as I was to find answers, and I took comfort in that. I decided that when they got older, Billy and Anne would have to do their own inquiry and find their own answers.

I also learned that I liked meditation, finding it calming, and used it later in life. Being with the group was a wonderful experience. I grew in new ways, becoming a more informed and open person and parent.

The group gave me respect for who I was as a single parent and nurtured me in my efforts. I was the outlier in the group, the only member who did not have a partner. That status can be killing—social invitations can dry up; your presence isn't always welcome; you become forgotten in the scheme of things. They welcomed and supported me. I was one of them. I was always grateful for their treatment of me and never took it for granted. It was also a morale booster when my marriage was floundering and when it ended. This unique group was there for me when I most needed help.

CHAPTER 26

The Reckoning

※ ※ ※

In late summer, Margaret called me. She asked me to meet her at a local coffee shop, telling me, "I've been thinking about our marriage and divorce and wanted to talk with you. I really take full responsibility for the breakdown of our marriage, for what I did. I am sorry for the way I treated you, and if we talk about what was going on for me, it might help you. It might help me cope with my guilt, too. I'd like both of us to understand and learn from what happened."

"Yes, of course," I said. I was surprised by the call—I hadn't talked with Margaret for months—and by her message.

We met for a long conversation. She said, "It wasn't your fault. You did everything you could. I was so threatened by closeness, so scared of intimacy, that I couldn't respond. I've had a pattern of conquest, of attracting men and then pulling back, rejecting them. I've seen that in men I've dated since we separated. I treated you the same way. When I start getting close, especially sexually, I get frightened and pull away. The coming and going is a long-standing pattern."

"You didn't do that with me before we got married. We were close in every way."

"I did love you but got scared right after we were married. You loved me and had expectations—I couldn't deal with that. And going to counseling with Shirley was too threatening. I used you to replace the family I had and lost. I suggested we get married because I was afraid I'd lose you, too. I feel guilty about that."

She told me she had realized that she was hostile to men and that it came from the way she felt about her father. "He was cold, dominating, scary. It's partly in reaction to my mother's attitudes and behaviors toward him, too. She's got some responsibility in this. I treated you the same way my mother treated my father."

I listened to what she said and then asked, "How did you get these insights?

"I got counseling and mostly talked with a male friend—it's platonic. The insights have come out in the last two months, but the problem is long-standing. Having these insights hasn't really changed my behavior. Maybe down the road. We had to get a divorce. There wasn't any other thing to do."

"What if I had held out longer despite the pain, your rejection?"

"Don't torture yourself. You did all you could. I'm not ready now and probably won't be for a long time."

What she said made sense to me. It helped to explain why our marriage had failed. I felt relieved, although I wasn't so sure the fault was only hers. She moved the conversation to our children.

"I realize that Anne was just being a normal seven-year-old. I overreacted to her. There might have been some competition between her and me, but that wasn't the real issue. Billy may not have known it, but I did care about him. He's a sensitive guy. Jack liked him, too. He calls him his brother. He is confused. He calls you his stepfather, too—you were a very good stepfather to him. I've been giving him special attention."

"I loved you and wanted to be married to you and be Jack's stepfather. I really liked him. But later from you—mostly contempt, no respect."

"I did respect you, but I know I didn't show it."

"No, you didn't. After the separation, when I was with you I wanted to hold you, and when I wasn't I was hurt and angry. But I wasn't a masochist. I had to end things. Thank you for calling me this week, for sharing your insights with me. I'm grateful."

This conversation opened up old wounds. That night I couldn't stop crying, shaking. I hadn't fully let go of my feelings about her: love, anger, frustration, grief. But the meeting was the goodbye we hadn't had before—one with mutual respect, understanding, and regard. I thought she had been astonishingly giving to me. Such kindness and courage. How many ex-wives or ex-husbands do what she did? In time, it helped me forgive her, accept my losses, and move on. I hoped that she could resolve her anguish and find inner peace. I don't know whether she ever did.

My conversation with Margaret, and the divorce that preceded it, reminded me of my limitations as a marriage partner. She had taken full responsibility for our failed relationship, but I knew I hadn't met her needs, either. I tried to overcome these limitations when I dated or engaged in a relationship with someone new. I got some feedback from women I dated that I still needed to communicate better: talk less, ask questions, listen more, be attentive to feelings—theirs and mine.

I dated more women who didn't fit the look I had long been drawn to. How many women might have I have met and possibly married if I had done that earlier? I'll never know. Letting go of a preference—an ideal of attractiveness—should have been easier, but it wasn't. I thought, too, that if I did become involved in a future serious relationship, I would do what so many mature men and women do: take my time, take my time, take my time. Get to know my partner in as many ways as possible before getting married. It's such a simple, even simplistic, notion. But diving ahead can be hard to resist, especially if you've been alone or lonely for a long time.

Introducing these changed attitudes in romantic relationships would take me more time and practice. What I was committed to doing, if I married again, was building a partnership that worked for both of us, one in which we shared financial resources, parenting or stepparenting responsibilities, family and friendship circles, eldercare, if necessary, while finding private time for ourselves. The fullness of life.

I also recognized that there aren't any assurances of marital success, that risks occur in any choices we make, and there is some mystery about how and why we fall in love with or are drawn to a partner whom we wish to marry. Some things we can look forward to and plan for, and others are surprises.

While participating in the training course offered by the Landmark Forum, I had reflected on my relationship issues with women and especially with Sue. Much later, I decided to write Sue a letter, which became, as I drafted it, a letter of thanks to her. In part, it reads:

I am writing to come to terms with our relationship, to accept all of what we had and what we lost and to recognize what you have meant to me. I'm blessed that, in the best and the hardest of times, you made and kept a loving commitment to me, to our marriage, and to your role as mother of Billy and Anne. At this point in my life, I think of you as "one of a kind," unusual for your warmth, sensitivity, and caring—the woman and wife against whom I measure all others. I didn't always think that, but I believe now that this has been so. I only wish we had had more time to weave our lives, and those of Billy and Anne, together. I think we would have been effective parents—better than I was alone—and happy ones.

Thank you for treating me as a full partner in our marriage, for letting me share in raising and caring for our children, in maintaining our home, and in collaborating as host for our social activities with family and friends. There was no competitiveness between us.

Thank you for introducing me to your extended family that has been a life force for the children and me for over 20 years. Without them, we would be so much poorer.

Thank you for showing me the value of cultivating and sustaining friendships over long periods of time. Before I met you, I didn't understand the value of this. Now I try to practice what you modeled so well.

Thank you for being my best friend. We could talk about anything and did. We shared common interests and acted on them—more than I've experienced with anyone since.

I want to ask you, too, for your forgiveness. There were times when I didn't listen to you enough or really empathize with you, times when I didn't know how to fully love you when you needed or expected it. I am so sorry that I let you down in those and other moments.

I am sorry that at times I was impatient and very judgmental in relating to you and frequently dismissive of our marriage problems as "your problems." If "you'd shape up," things would be okay, I thought. I didn't reflect on or fully realize how I may have contributed to our problems. You deserved better than that.

On the other hand, you rarely, if ever, criticized me for my limitations or failures. You were a generous and accepting person, a kind spirit who I knew loved me and wanted the best for me.

If you were here, I would promise to do the best I could to be your faithful husband, lover, and best friend. I would be straight with you about our issues. I am better now, I hope, at these things than I was when you were alive. If I have changed for the better, I hope, too, that that would help you feel happy about your life and happy with me.

I miss you, dear Sue. I love you still. May your life be full wherever you are.

By the time I composed this letter to Sue, she had been dead over twenty years, and my divorce from Margaret had occurred over ten years earlier. Much of its content, though, spoke to the issues that I thought were important both in these past relationships and in new ones that I anticipated. My goal was to be a better husband and partner, someone more aware of my own strengths and weaknesses, if I got the chance.

CHAPTER 27

A Call for Help

❋ ❋ ❋

A few months after my conversation with Margaret, I got another telephone call I hadn't expected. One of my mom's neighbors had heard noises and what she thought were cries coming from my mom's apartment, but she couldn't get ahold of her. She asked me to come over.

When I entered Mom's apartment, I found her in her bed, unable to get up, writhing in pain. "Tim, Tim, help me. My back hurts so bad. I tried to go to the bathroom, but I can't move without the pain. I've been here for hours. Please, please, get me some help," she said.

I used her bedroom phone to call 911 and sat on the edge of the bed, holding her hand, as we waited for the paramedics to come. Her teeth were clenched, her eyes mostly closed. When the paramedics arrived, they wheeled a cart into the bedroom, checked Mom's vital signs, and gently lifted her onto the cart. They took her down two flights of stairs and transferred her into their van. I sat next to her. She was alert but very quiet.

We didn't talk to each other on the way to the hospital. I couldn't help remembering the paramedics coming to the house when Sue died.

The ER doctors diagnosed Mom with cracked vertebrae—small fissures, they called it—in her lower back, almost surely caused by the onset of osteoporosis. With her consent, they arranged for her to be transferred to a nursing home in St. Paul, which had an opening and adequate staff to handle her needs. I left her as she was falling asleep in the ER room with the help of a sedative.

Mom was a good patient, her physical therapist told me. She did all the required exercises and a few extra repetitions as well. "She kind of likes the attention," he said, smiling. "There's a good chance she can get out of here in three weeks—a lot faster than most folks who have her kind of problem."

Sure enough, three weeks after she was admitted, she walked out the front doors of the nursing home, using a cane but with her shoulders back, head up straight. I took her picture. She looked determined and wasn't smiling.

This episode was my introduction to eldercare. I didn't know it then, but I had become a member of the "sandwich generation," people raising children and taking care of their aging parents or family members at the same time. During the next fourteen years before entering a nursing home for the last time, Mom would need a lot more help from me. I was the only one of her adult kids living in her hometown—Jim lived in Omaha— which required that I be the primary caregiver. I didn't resent that. After all, she'd been there for Billy, Anne, and me.

Giving her support did not come at the expense of finding time to parent my children, which can happen in single-parent families, but it made managing daily activities more challenging. I had to have Billy watch Anne more often, and I asked both kids to do more things for themselves—laundry, pet care, yardwork. I don't remember them complaining when I left them to help their nana. They had experienced her good side and cared about her.

For my part, I stayed in touch with Mom through telephone calls and occasional unannounced visits, but the most effective approach to helping her was our weekly Saturday-afternoon visits. She created an agenda and I drove her and stayed with her until she finished her shopping trips, usually a three- to four-hour run.

On our first trips, I was astonished at how much time she spent shopping for what she wanted. It seemed to me that she took forever eyeing options before making a selection, whether for skin cream or orange juice or a window curtain. Eventually I realized that while her shopping accomplished practical goals, its more important purpose was to connect her with her surroundings, with people, with life itself. She could use her body and challenge her mind for good reasons. Saturday-afternoon shop-ping freed her from her isolation and energized her. Why hurry?

Still, my role was limited, and time often passed slowly. Before long, I chose a middle road: I often found a quiet spot in the store and meditated while she shopped. I sat on chairs, low-level display risers, and occasional-ly a floor when slipping into meditation. For a while I could hear people's voices, their footsteps, the store music, and then all was quiet. Before I began, I asked Mom whether she needed my help and, if not, whether she was okay with my meditation practice. I told her where I would be and that if she needed something to just nudge me. I skipped meditation when I thought she needed me. But otherwise my practice sustained and refreshed me.

Afterward, she and I talked about my meditation practice and she told me about her dreams. It brought us closer. We continued our Saturday shopping trips until she had to use a wheelchair and was too frail to travel in my car. I can still remember the little smile on her face as she clutched her shopping bags and entered her apartment.

In the same year that Mom first entered the nursing home for physical therapy, my dad died. Since he was living in Los Angeles, there was no call to me for help. His wife and my half-sister and half-brother were there for him. He died from heart disease, driven by many factors. Much of his résumé and biography was exceptional: great athlete, successful radio personality, engaging raconteur, a person everyone wanted to be with. But the story behind the public personality was checkered: a working alcohol-ic, abusive to his wives and children, lonely and angry until he died. He was a contradiction, a public man lost at home.

On the plane ride to Los Angeles, I thought of my history with him. One memory stayed with me more than others.

When a high school friend of his wanted to leave Minnesota for LA—to leave the cold for a new start—Dad loaned him airfare, which his friend couldn't afford. Almost fifty years later, when Dad was sixty-five and re-tired, he left Minnesota for LA for the same reasons. Once there, he con-tacted his old friend for job leads. His friend was head of the AFL-CIO, the largest union in LA. One of the union's insurance salesmen, who re-ported to him, had recently retired. Dad's friend transferred the retired man's clientele group to dad, setting him up with an immediate job, good income, and respect.

Dad adapted to his new job by buying an older white Cadillac, white slacks and golf shirt, and a pair of soft, white leather shoes—white bucks. On his work calls, he was ready with a hearty handshake and engaging conversation for his union brothers and sisters. I smiled as I remembered his personal rejuvenation. He had reincarnated himself for public consumption.

My stepmother, my two brothers, our sister, and I attended his Roman Catholic funeral mass and burial service. As I listened to the priest's homily—based chiefly on information about Dad that Jim had provided—I recognized what a talented, affecting person Dad was, but I didn't miss him. I didn't feel much sense of loss. The distance between us was real and long-standing and couldn't be reconciled.

Later, as the priest read a final burial prayer at the grave site, a huge airplane flew directly above us, drowning out the sounds of his words.

CHAPTER 28

Billy and Anne: Growing Up

When I came back from my dad's funeral, I had lunch with a friend whose kids were about the same age as Billy and Anne. We talked about how our parenting might need to change now that they were older, but we weren't quite sure what we would do the same and what differently. After I got home, I sat on the front steps of our house and thought about the conversation. Two parents rode by on their bikes with one small child in a bike seat and a second child on her own bike. It made me think back to biking with Billy and Anne when they were younger.

Back then, my parenting was influenced by people like Benjamin Spock, Rudolf Dreikurs, and Alfred Adler. Even though the kids were now older, many of those experts' ideas and approaches still made sense to me: Encourage a feeling of belonging. Develop trusting relationships. Create regular routines, but don't be too rigid. Ensure consequences for behaviors. Promote a sense of community. Be a caring presence. Sustain your commitments.

I believed those principles had helped my kids build a positive sense of self, openness to others, and resilient attitudes—not perfect behaviors, but healthy ones. The trick was figuring out how to adapt these ideas as they grew older.

I decided that the kids should continue doing their family and household chores—continue existing routines, if not necessarily on the same days and at the same times as they had done them before. They washed their own clothes and, most of the time, kept their rooms tidy. They helped care for Teddy and Joey, our cats, and Max, our sheltie. They watered the grass, raked leaves, and shoveled snow. Billy kept up his neighborhood paper route, and Anne helped me with grocery and other shopping. They observed nightly curfews. I gave them weekly allowances, which I increased over time.

That fall, Billy continued to quarterback his park league football team. I watched him play. In one game, he intercepted two passes, which he ran back for touchdowns—extraordinary plays. After the game, he wasn't too old to accept a hug from me.

Billy's favorite sport was football, but he tried other team sports for the first time. Over two summers, he played Babe Ruth League baseball as an outfielder. He wore his uniform with pride and usually a smile before heading to his games. He joined a church-league basketball team, followed by a year on his high school B-squad team. He also learned how to downhill ski in a club sponsored by his school.

With my workload and Anne to watch, I couldn't get to many of his baseball and basketball games, but he and I still connected through sports. In warm weather, we often passed a football to each other on our street, at parks, and wherever we could when we vacationed.

Once in Maine, our friend Brad, a high school football coach and school athletic director, let us practice on the beautiful football field his team used. It was before the start of the season, and the grass was green, fresh, and mowed. It was quiet. We were the only people in the stadium. I loved running pass patterns for Billy, whose throws seemed always to be on target.

Occasionally we went to a Vikings game. During winters, we took weekend skiing breaks in Wisconsin or Minnesota. It was easy being with Billy—he was open-minded, friendly, and cooperative. I was grateful for our time together, for the trusting relationship we had.

His interest in music exploded, mostly for heavy metal and punk rock bands. He went to concerts at the Minneapolis Armory, sometimes joining others near the stage and once in a while letting himself be passed over the hands and heads of the crowd. "It's safe, Dad, it really is," he'd say when he got home. I talked with other parents about this kind of activity, which their kids had experienced, and we all decided it was okay.

For a short time, he tried learning the bass guitar, and I would hear him practice while I was in our kitchen making dinner. But he discovered that listening to music was a bigger draw than attempting to make it.

After having an exceptional teacher—Mr. Hauer—in sixth grade at his elementary school, he didn't find a junior high school teacher with whom he really clicked. He wasn't excited about going to school, but he didn't complain about it, either. He got satisfactory grades. Some of the friends he made in school were kids of color, who made up about half of his schoolmates—a significant difference from his elementary school. In time, he brought them home to hang out.

One spring at his junior high, he joined a large group of both white students and students of color in a protest against a new dress code: no hip-hop styles (bandanas, fat laces, or baseball caps) and no punk rock clothes. The students rolled through the hallways and spilled outside onto the grounds and nearby street. One of them had alerted TV reporters. The story made the local nightly news, and there were follow-up stories in the Minneapolis and greater Minnesota papers. Their demonstration also attracted the attention of Minneapolis police, who watched but didn't intervene.

"There weren't really leaders, just too many of us to handle. It was all of us," Billy told me.

School administrators adjusted their initial ban. They said that in the future they would seek more feedback from parents and students before they made critical policy changes. I learned of the demonstration after the fact, but I wouldn't have opposed it, as long as Billy made up for lost class time. He was connecting with kids who were different from him in something that counted.

His motivation to attend school and study varied. He was a late bloomer, and many kids at school and on the football team were growing up faster than he was. When he was in eighth grade, we sought advice from our family doctor, who said that Billy's growth spurt would come in about a year. Billy told me that waiting through that next year was "like a lifetime, something that was never going to end."

He was conscious, too, that he was one of the few kids who did not have either a mother or a stepmother in his life, a loving woman to talk with about the changes he was experiencing. He had his grandparents, other family members, and me, but he felt different from the other kids. At times he was frustrated, was angry, and vented, but he didn't act out regularly or treat others poorly.

In the summer following eighth grade, he, his cousin Brett, Grandpa Ad, and I made a trip to the cabin. The boys went fishing with Ad, helped me make meals, and many times sat on the dock in conversation. I saw them gesturing and laughing, hands in the air. I remembered them as three-year-olds running on top of the roof, bringing Uncle Bart and me nails for the shingling work we were doing. I was glad they were sharing their private time, two boys with a similar history on the edge of adolescence.

It would be decades before we hosted Brett at the cabin again. But in his middle and high school years, Billy built relationships of immediate and lasting importance with guys from different parts of the city. Later he would invite some of them, along with neighborhood friends, for weekend visits to the cabin.

At home, Billy was nearly always cooperative. He wasn't rebellious, nor did he challenge our family rules on chores, curfews, and other matters. He distanced himself from Anne and me in understandable ways, heading for private time in his room or outside. He could be down or unpredictable, like other junior high kids. I was aware of his frustrations but thought he was handling them in a reasonable way. He grew more independent, but I didn't feel rejected by him. I laughed when he later told me that he was "hermetically sealed in my age bracket, but didn't have a case of dad-itis—'I can't be seen with my Dad.'"

During this time, as Anne moved through the higher elementary grades, she continued playing park league soccer, won parts in after-school theater productions, and got along okay most of the time with her older brother. She was taller than other girls her age and smart, pretty, friendly, open, and funny. She kept her school friends from earlier grades and, like Billy, began making new friends who were often kids of color. Our neighborhood public schools brought children of many races together.

Anne held her first sleepover birthday parties with kids her age and some from our neighborhood who were older. Billy had had his sleepovers with several friends, but Anne's were full productions—seven to eight friends in sleeping bags on our living room floor with loud storytelling, multiple pizza servings, and pillow fights.

At her first overnight, before lights out, one of the older girls gently and patiently combed out Anne's hair, as a mother would, I thought—as her mother would have done. After midnight, I had to visit at least a couple of times to quiet the group. "Oh, yes, Mr. Delmont, we're going to sleep, no more talking for sure, for sure," they said. I heard them as I walked up the stairs to my bedroom—little peals of laughter, snatches of conversation, more laughter, the sounds of young voices, comfortable in the moment and with each other. And then it was quiet.

I loved having Anne's friends over. They brought energy, fun, spontaneity, caring—good vibes for her and for me.

Like her brother, Anne invited many friends to the cabin and made new ones there. They canoed, swam, played volleyball, and horsed around, at ease in the friendly climate she created. Later she invited her high school and college friends for annual visits. Mekenok was a place of community for her, for Billy, and for me—a family tradition we sustained.

At her elementary school, Anne's teachers told me she was an excellent student with a friendly presence. Mr. Hauer, who had taught Billy, often asked her to carry out leadership tasks. He recognized and encouraged Anne as he had Billy. He was the kind of teacher I wished all kids could have.

Anne pushed back little on the boundaries I set, did her chores, and participated willingly in our family activities. She seemed to be a healthy, happy child. I parented her with what I thought was a light touch. I trusted her. She was on the cusp of middle school but hadn't yet begun pulling away from me, creating the physical and personal distance that would come later. In those years, I hardly worried about her at all.

Still, I wasn't entirely sure how well I was doing as her parent. I was grateful when she later told me about some of her memories of my parenting at that time

"I thought your job was to take care of me," she said. "You made dinner, you encouraged me, you liked me, you invited my friends over, you set boundaries, kind of handled Billy and me separately—protected our privacy. The good thing for me was that I didn't even think about it."

When Billy was finishing his freshman year at Washburn High School, I proposed a father-and-son trip I thought in a few years he might not want to do—now was the time. I had saved money for it. I told him we could go any place in the country he wanted to over his spring break.

Billy chose New York City because we could visit Brett and his parents, who lived in New Jersey, and because he wanted to experience America's other huge, famous city besides Los Angeles, which he'd already visited. Later, when Anne was a teenager, I made the same offer to her. In her case, she and I and three of her friends visited her Granny Irene and Grandpa Ad in Tucson, Arizona, with a side trip to Nogales, Mexico.

Before Billy and I headed to New York, I rented a hotel room for us in Manhattan's theater district. There was so much to experience in the city, most of it new to both of us. We took the Circle Line boat ride around Manhattan with tourists from all over the world. We visited the United Nations building. We had the best pastrami sandwiches we'd ever eaten in a Times Square deli, went to see the New York Knicks play, and visited Chinatown.

Some experiences in the Bronx were unexpected: the sight of a man sitting in the window of a walkup apartment shooting up drugs, groups of people warming themselves with street wastebasket fires or walking through the rubble of huge numbers of open lots—all visible from our seats on the elevated train to the Bronx Zoo. A visit to the top of the Empire State Building gave us a view of the density and massiveness of the city, a final, unforgettable perspective.

As we walked back to our hotel, Billy said, "New York is fantastic. I'm so glad we came. I like Minneapolis, but I could see myself here, too, when I'm older." I told him that was a possibility, especially with family nearby.

On Easter weekend, we took the train to Princeton, New Jersey. Uncle Bart invited Billy and Brett to help him on his Christmas tree farm, where the boys dug places for tree seedlings, planted and watered them, and cleaned up the fields and barns. Billy liked the farm work—a respite from the pace of the week in the city. With Bart's family, we cooked, shared stories, and, with wine and apple cider, toasted Sue.

On Billy's birthday, Cindy, Billy's aunt, made a carrot cake. "Have some, Billy," she said. "It was one of your Mom's favorites."

Billy's birthday that year fell on Easter Sunday, ten years after Sue had passed. When Sue died, I wondered how her death would change Billy's and Anne's lives. In the ten years that followed, I tried to do my best for my children: set expectations and boundaries, nurture and support them, hold them accountable, be dependable and fair-minded, let them know they counted. None of that changed as they grew up. Nothing I did as a parent fully compensated for the loss of their mother when they were small and vulnerable, nor when they were growing older, but I hoped they knew I was always there for them.

As Billy and Anne grew older, I still carried many of the parenting expectations of their earlier years, but I modified them, too. I offered Billy what he later called a "hugely expansive leash from the house." I allowed him to take airplane rides by himself to visit his relatives. To ride his bike alone for a number of blocks to his sports practices. To bike over two miles to a suburban recreation center for daylong swimming and diving activities. To skateboard to or play in areas beyond our neighborhood. To deliver newspapers by himself. To attend rock concerts unescorted. I believed that one of my tasks as a parent was to offer my kids opportunities to make their decisions in situations of increasing risk that I believed they were mature enough to handle.

I was not going to be a helicopter parent, one in control of their lives who made nearly all decisions for them. I wanted them to learn from any mistakes they made and to gain confidence in their ability to make meaningful decisions. At the same time, I didn't feel I ever gave up my parental authority.

Another major decision I made was continuing to invest our money and my time in activities I thought promoted their growth and development. Their participation in team sports, music lessons, activities with friends, and travels with family topped the list.

Like other parents I knew, I drove both kids to their after-school, evening, and weekend activities, whose numbers mushroomed. At times, the driving seemed endless. But the kids were my captives, too, and some of our best conversations happened on those very private drives. Away from friends, they often shared their inner thoughts and feelings about school experiences, family issues, or other matters. I felt I was staying in the loop at least some of the time.

As Billy and Anne widened their friendship circles, I wanted them to feel that our home was a welcoming place for their friends. In our wedding service, Sue and I had said about our home, "Let there be a spirit of hospitality and acceptance for all who come." Maintaining that notion in practice with noisy, unpredictable elementary, junior high, and high school kids was a challenge, but I couldn't imagine not doing it. Our home and neighborhood were Billy's and Anne's, not just mine.

Through their school and park activities, the kids made many friendships, some of them, as mentioned, with kids of color. These activities opened the door for me to connect and make friends with their families. When I coached Anne's park league softball team, a number of my players were black and Hispanic. Their parents and relatives came to our games, which were held in parks throughout the city. Later, I served for two years as president of Anne's high school PTA, in which I worked together with black parents, in particular, on school problems.

From these experiences, I learned about the patterns of prejudice, in policies and practices, that existed in our schools and in our city and the pain they brought to families of color. From direct involvement with these families, I learned, too, about the specific obstacles they faced in their everyday lives. My kids had moved beyond our neighborhood bubble, and I had, too.

I expanded my consulting and teaching jobs, negotiating time away from my University of Minnesota office from four days to three days on campus so I could have more flexibility in managing my family's increasing commitments and activities. The money I made was about the same as when I had worked five days a week at the university, but the freedom I experienced was wonderful. I was there for the kids more often while taking care of family and household responsibilities. And I engaged more fully in community affairs.

I also dated less, giving more time to the kids and providing care for my mother's needs. I didn't find a Sue or a Liz or a Margaret. I didn't know whether I would. My life looked to me like that of other single parents I knew, all of whom were women. Our duties and aspirations seemed about the same, even if our genders weren't. Our children's needs came first, and the rest followed.

Anne with Eldora,
our nanny for five
years

On the beach in
Ocean Park, Maine,
with, from left to
right, members of the
Roberts family and us:
Merry, Billy, Betsy,
me, Chrissy, Anne,
and Lindsay

Billy and
Grandpa Bob
Dunbar

Anne and I watched Billy play quarterback many times for his park league football team.

Billy won the most valuable player award in his football team's playoff game.

The kids and their friend Frankenstein at the Los Angeles Universal Studios Amusement Park

Hard to beat wave riding in Long Beach, California

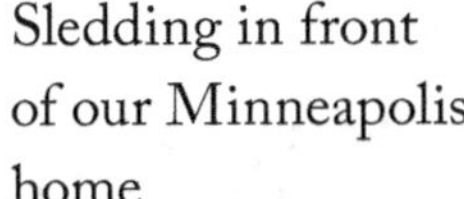

Sledding in front of our Minneapolis home

My mother, Betty, known as Nana, and Anne

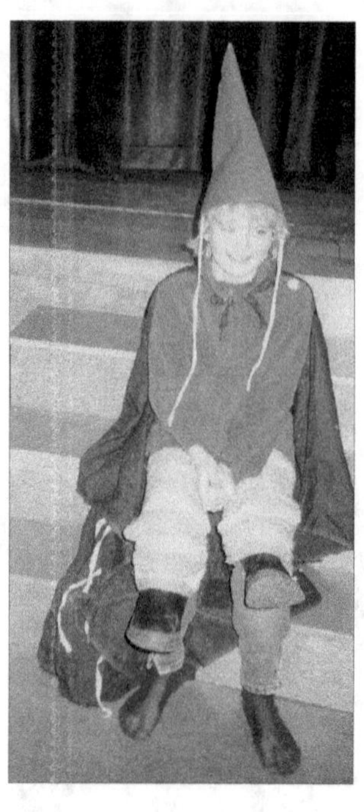

Anne in costume for a
park theater production

Anne and her park
league softball teammates
survived my coaching,
winning most of their
games.

Anne, age ten, and
her friends at her first
birthday sleepover

From left to right, top row, our Meditation Group: Jean, Neil, Nancy, Tom, Ron, Joe, Iva, me, Carol, and Doris. Rich took the photo.

Over ten years, we grew in different ways.

CHAPTER 29

The Long View

❋ ❋ ❋

I wasn't very well prepared for my time as a dad. What I didn't know far exceeded what I did. I had few models among male peers to emulate. I scrambled to stay on top of the flow of parenting roles and responsibilities. I changed my perspectives and behaviors to cope with parenting needs and dilemmas that emerged. I was like other single parents I met.

When Sue died, my most immediate goal was caring for Billy and Anne. I built a family team to accomplish that goal, understanding that I was the person most responsible for parenting the kids, but at that time I had no real grasp of how much help I would need. Most importantly, four of the children's grandparents stepped up. Having been single parents themselves in earlier eras, they shared with me some of what they had done. By taking care of my children and nurturing me, they made it possible for me to find my way.

I could hardly believe how committed they were. Growing up, I had had almost no meaningful contact with my own grandparents. As a child, I lived with one grandfather through much of elementary school until his death, but I can't remember having a single conversation with him or doing anything together. Both of my grandmothers were dead, and the remaining grandfather—my dad's father, Nick—mostly chose to stay away.

I did my best to sustain our relationships with my kid's grandparents, with the exception of my dad. That included providing eldercare for three of them, in state and out. My experience came full circle: I tried to return the care to them that they had willingly given to the children and me when we were most in need. We made and kept a worthy bargain, one that I hadn't anticipated.

Sue's extended family in New Jersey and Maine also supported us. They welcomed our visits and let us know how much they cared about us. Billy, Anne, and I kept in touch by writing letters, sending Christmas gifts, and visiting them frequently. Building and continuing our relationships with them over a decade involved setting priorities—on their part and on ours—and finding travel dollars, neither of which was easy. I tried to follow Sue's example in sustaining selective, long-term relationships with out-of-state family members. It was well worth it.

I experienced other surprises, too: help came to us from many quarters. Finding Eldora, our longtime nanny, was a godsend, as were the contributions of most of the nannies before her. Their help over the first six years of my single parenting stabilized our home environment. It was never easy to find nannies, but with help from Sue's mother, we did it. I tried my best to pay fair wages, understand their needs, and treat them with respect and courtesy. I wanted them to value their time with us.

Neighbors and friends in Minneapolis, in the meditation group, and on Mekenok Island were also a huge resource for me. I didn't cultivate a lot of close adult friendships—the most notable exception being my longtime friend Roger—but I shared as much time as possible with these folks, especially other parents with kids. I invited them to be with us, and we went where they were. I told them, "Watch out if you invite us—we are coming!" And we did.

I couldn't have raised small children by myself and worked for pay without the ongoing help of family, nannies, and friends—people who consistently carried out key nurturing and supportive roles.

In raising my children, I also recognized how important it was to have access to free or affordable public and nonprofit services in our community. We built our lives around many of them: neighborhood daycare services; preschool and full-time elementary education programs; park and playground after-school and summer team sports, exercise, and arts activities; library visits for books, movies, and records; and physical, dental, and mental health services and counseling. Not all communities offer such a rich mix of quality, affordable services.

I was also fortunate to work for two universities—the University of Minnesota and St. Mary's University—that offered family-friendly policies. They provided adequate salaries and crucial benefits, such as healthcare coverage, vacation, and sick days. My bosses approved many adjustments to my work schedules that I requested. Such policies were not the norm among employers in that era, and since they were so important to me and broke new ground for my employers, I carried them out with as much integrity as possible. I wanted to show my bosses that the risks they were taking in changing their workplace environment worked for them as well as for me. For ten years, none of my bosses eliminated or changed these policies. Both sides were satisfied with the deals we struck.

During this period, I had less opportunity to pursue personal interests, but I didn't entirely give them up. Each year, I also used all my earned vacation time from my job to spend time with the kids at our cabin as well as travel to visit family. On these trips, others parented the kids for me so that I could have a break from my everyday duties. Time relaxing by myself or with others was an important factor in attempting to maintain work/life balance over many years.

In parenting Billy and Anne, there was another especially important factor at play: the kids did not experience the childhood diseases, serious illnesses, ongoing disabilities, or debilitating accidents that other children did. Eldora and I brought them to our local family practice and dental offices for required vaccinations and regular checkups. Without significant health challenges, the kids participated fully in family events, school activities, and community educational and recreational opportunities. Preventive medicine, accessible healthcare services, and a little luck carried the day for us.

Like the kids, I was healthy, too. Regular exercise helped, often with the children at the YWCA and outdoors. I benefited from many caring, supportive relationships that lessened my stress as a single father, contributed to the resilience I tried to build, and gave me confidence that I could carry out my single parenting duties. Over time, our being healthy was a huge plus—one that I did not take for granted.

I recognized, too, that regardless of any challenges I faced as a single father, the kids and I lived in a privileged fashion. In our affluent white neighborhood we did not experience the poverty, crime, and discrimination that often characterized the lives of other single-parent families in Minnesota and elsewhere. In particular, I could afford the help of nannies as well as count on the support of family and friends—resources not routinely available to other single parents.

Still, being a single father was a difficult experience. The support I received did not save me from my own mistakes and misjudgments nor lessen the demands of the role. I felt on call 24/7. Unless the kids were with their grandparents or friends, there wasn't much slowdown or freedom in my schedule. Getting groceries, cooking, doing laundry, driving to activities, making to-do lists, attending to family relationships—managing our lives—usually took more time than I anticipated, even when Billy and Anne helped. I consistently felt the pressures and stresses of meeting the children's and my own needs.

Many family members and friends complimented me on my parenting, which I appreciated. But I still worried about things I didn't think I handled well, experiences that might affect them negatively as they grew out of childhood.

One was their feelings of loss from their mother's death. Both Billy and Anne appeared to be active, happy, confident children, and I didn't see consistent negative behaviors that might have signaled that they were having trouble coping with this traumatic experience. I wondered, though, whether I was missing signs, whether I didn't have the sensitivity to perceive pain they were experiencing but not overtly expressing.

I thought at the time that the chief purpose of family counseling was to address and solve problems. As a result, I may have missed opportunities that could have been beneficial for them and for me. Their mom, because of her training as a social worker, might have seen things differently and acted, if I had been the one who died. It was also true that they lost a stepmother. I thought their relationships with Margaret were checkered at best—some support, but very little consistent nurturing. But I may have missed that that loss had significant impact on them, too. Again, I passed on the opportunity to get proactive counseling after our divorce, which might have been a mistake.

A powerful reality was that, over the ten-year period following Sue's death, I did not develop a loving marriage or long-term relationship with a new partner. There was no nurturing stepmother for Billy and Anne. I had anticipated a different experience for them and for me. Not finding a caring, committed partner was my biggest disappointment.

I had misgivings, too, over not having reached out to other members of my mom's or dad's extended family to develop relationships. I had reasons for not doing so, but I never knew whether I had denied Billy and Anne experiences that might have helped them grow and develop or led to productive relationships for them later in their lives.

During this period, I also failed at finding a church home for the kids and me. A huge number of families, headed by couples or single parents, discover their faith and build important relationships in their church communities. They may have positive, life-changing experiences while being supported in many ways by their faith partners. There was a hole in our spiritual and religious history, one my kids had to address for themselves later.

Single parenting involved managing what seemed like a huge number of family activities. It required accepting important changes in our lives, many of which I hadn't anticipated. We made progress, but there were times when I thought I let the kids down. Sometimes I felt I didn't change quickly enough or well enough to be the father they deserved. I felt these ambiguous feelings over many, many years and still have them.

In writing this book, I gained new perspectives on my parenting that I hadn't thought of before. One is how important each child is—mine and others. I was in the delivery room when Billy was born. Shortly after Sue gave birth to Anne by cesarean section, I saw her in the hospital nursery. Not long after their births, I held each baby in my arms. These experiences were incredible and life-changing. But as my kids grew, my feelings about them became deeper, stronger. The night I fed baby Anne her bottle, spoke to her—almost face-to-face—as she looked directly into my eyes and smiled, I felt a connection that I will always remember. Telling Billy that his mother had died, his arms around my neck, with grayness and cold winds all about us, was the same kind of moment, the same kind of deep feeling. I will never forget the look on that sweet boy's face.

The longer I was a single parent, the more I wanted to give them what they seemed to need. "It's not about me; it's about them" became a driving motivation for me.

I felt blessed with the relationship I developed with both of my kids starting when they were small. There was something special between us—the shared experience of loss and love—that would not disappear. Three decades have passed, and I feel as committed to each one as I did when they were children. Each was still important as an adolescent and now as an adult. The notion that we are parents for life is not a cliché; it is a welcome reality. I think if we fully parent our children when they are little—because they deserve it—we are likely to build lifelong relationships that we all value.

The intentionality I felt about parenting helped me discern the purposes of my adult life. I really wanted to have it all: be an available, effective parent, have a successful career, and find a loving partner. I thought it was worth a try. Those closest to us often said that they thought the kids and I were doing fine. Much of the time, I thought we were, too. I carried out several demanding administrative jobs while teaching courses and building a consulting practice. My second marriage failed, but I dated and made friends with women who helped me understand more about my fathering efforts and myself. Trying to have it all stretched and rewarded me in ways I hadn't anticipated. I'm glad I made the effort.

My attempt to have it all also spoke to something deep inside me. I realized that we only have so much time to discover who we are and what gives meaning to our lives. I wanted to use my time as fully and successfully as I could. Being a single father may or may not have been my calling, but it challenged me to find my best self.

Sue's death was a traumatic event for Billy, Anne, and me—one whose impact we would feel, in varying degrees, throughout our lives. Over time, I came to see problems in family life, work, and romantic relationships through the lens of her death. I thought that I could address emerging problems, solve some, and avoid being overwhelmed by others, because "no one died": none of these problems were as consequential as her death had been.

I'm not sure whether this attitude helped me be more optimistic, but I know I was more accepting, less frustrated, and less anxious in the face of challenges than might otherwise have been the case. I felt calm, if not fully confident, in making difficult decisions. I thought my kids and I could deal with almost anything and survive it. I carried that attitude with me during their childhood, adolescence, and beyond. I carry it still.

At Sue's wake, my grandpa Nick said, "This is a terrible thing, Timmy, losing your young wife. But these little ones will give you back your life." He was right. I couldn't imagine—and still can't—a more powerful and worthwhile experience than the one I had.

I was prepared to be a single parent and carry out many roles, but not prepared enough. Various people helped me as I found my way. Out of necessity, my views of work, marriage, and family life evolved. I became better at parenting and finding work/life balance. I recognized at least some of my limitations as a husband and father, and I tried to improve in both roles.

I have been a father, a single father, a stepfather, and now a grandfather. I am grateful for the opportunities I have had to carry out fathering responsibilities over a long period of time, and I believe these experiences have deepened my life and made it more meaningful. And I am especially honored to have been an everyday father, a role for me of lasting value.

Epilogue

❋ ❋ ❋

It has been over forty years since Sue died and my single parenting began. In this book, I have shared some of what my children and I experienced, especially in the first decade after her death. Following that decade, and my divorce from Margaret, I spent another fourteen years as a single parent. How the kids and I made it through their middle school, high school, and college experiences is a whole story in itself, but what follows are a few highlights.

Our relatives in Maine continue to be a draw for us. Little has changed there; the culture and beauty of the place remain. Some family members have died, but their children and grandchildren now welcome us. Social media helps us stay connected, too.

At Mekenok Island in northern Minnesota, we enjoy the lake, the land, our aging but updated cabin, and our vibrant community. Nearly all the senior island leaders whom we knew well have passed. They have been replaced by younger islanders, who nurture their families and neighborly friendships. It remains a rustic, atypical, but inviting vacation place for us.

The grandparents who introduced us to our Maine and Mekenok communities and supported my single parenting have passed. All lived into their late eighties. We learned from them how to live life fully, including coping—for well or ill—with the limitations of old age. Sue's family replaced my own in many ways. Over a very long period of time, I reached out to them and they reciprocated. Such a blessing.

Ad, Sue's stepfather, died first. Billy sat with him, on vigil, through many days and nights. On the night that Billy went home to sleep, Ad died peacefully. We scattered his ashes in a grassy area, filled with trees and bushes, on the edge of the golf course behind his longtime home in St. Paul. Although he was not a believer in an afterlife, it felt to us, as we distributed his ashes, that his spirit was with us.

Bob, Sue's biological father, slipped into Alzheimer's disease. When his letters and telephone calls from Los Angeles stopped, we grew worried about him, especially when he didn't return our calls. Billy and I visited him. In the middle of the day, we found him in his bathrobe, disheveled, his apartment a mess, the bathroom smelly. A check for $17,000, his share of a property sale completed by his family, was lying in a wastebasket, unendorsed.

Staff at the retirement community where he lived were not trained to meet his needs. Working with his sister, we found an attractive, affordable assisted living facility to which we moved him. Over the years, its staff gave us updates on his condition. When they found Bob alone wandering along city streets, window-shopping, they had to take away his privileges. A cheerful person, he died peacefully and was buried in Maine; we attended the graveside service. That trip was the only sad one I can remember making to this home away from home.

As my mom—Nana, to her grandchildren—aged, she coped resolutely with many diseases that limited her mobility and would ultimately take her life. She lived long enough to see her grandchildren grow into adulthood, staying connected with all of us.

After Ad died, Irene, Sue's mother, grew increasingly frail but retained her quick mind. She and I were the closest adults to Sue and were inextricably connected to each other because of it. Our relationship was more than son-in-law to mother-in-law. For me, she was a confidante and dear friend. At her memorial service, I said, "If you luck out, as I have, you may discover that your mother-in-law has become your friend for life. And if you are luckier yet, as I was, she may even turn into an 'equivalent parent'—a loving presence—who enriches your life in ways you needed but never expected." We spread her ashes in the same green space where we had Ad's, as she had requested.

When Sue died of cardiac arrhythmia in 1976, her doctor told me that the cause of her death was a mystery—one that frustrated and discouraged us. Findings of recent biomedical studies have linked cardiac arrhythmia with the condition of preeclampsia (previously called toxemia), which Sue experienced in the last stage of her pregnancy with Anne. Preeclampsia decreases the heart's ability to pump blood and makes it work harder, increasing the risk of heart failure. To offset the effects of preeclampsia, doctors now often prescribe oral or IV medications or induce labor. Sue was not given these medications, and she delivered nearly two weeks after her due date. Today she would have been treated far differently, perhaps narrowing or eliminating her risk of death—a stunning realization for us.

Billy now goes by Will. He has worked in governmental and educational positions and is married to Gaby, a preschool teacher. They live in Minneapolis with their two children, Paulina and Andrea. We get together regularly, sharing holiday and family milestones, our Mekenok cabin, and events in the Minneapolis community.

Anne is a psychotherapist in private practice. She and her husband, Todd, a chemical engineer, live in Minneapolis with their son, Wyatt. Like Will and his family, they live near me and remain fully in my life. I am grateful to have both of their families close by.

My brother, Jim, and sister, Laurie, supported the children and me in many ways, and we continue our visits and contact with them, as we do with our longtime Princeton family members, Val, Cary, and Brett.

I live in our house in the same Minneapolis neighborhood in which I raised Will and Anne. I regularly care for my grandchildren after school— what a delight! I tend to the house and yard, grow vegetables, and make sure the annual and perennial flowers are blooming. I volunteer for political campaigns and church activities, and sometimes I write. A few longtime neighbors are still here, and we hold the annual summer block party and occasional social gatherings to help us through our lives and, some would say, our long winters. Newcomers, who are mostly young couples with small children, are definitely welcome.

I am retired from my work as a higher education administrator, faculty member, and consultant. Later in my career, I was offered and accepted several jobs at the senior level in two universities. I climbed the ladder later than I expected but did not regret my career trajectory. I thought that if I had traded off a commitment to family life in favor of earlier career advancement, I and my children would have been worse off. Once opportunities for parenting our younger children are gone, what replaces them?

About twenty years ago, I met Jo, a professor and administrator at a local liberal arts college, who was a single parent raising two sons. She participated in a workshop I was co-leading, and at the end of the session, she approached me with a question. We began a discussion that continued through the lunch that followed. We talked almost exclusively about our single parenting experiences. Connection—and attraction—started immediately. When it was time for both of us to go, I asked her whether we could hug. She said yes. When I called her two days later with an offer for a picnic lunch at one of our city lakes, she said yes again! I was and am still thrilled that we found each other.

Jo and I married and have built the long, deep, loving relationship I always hoped I would find. I traded twenty-one years of single parenting for a new blended family. Her sons—my stepsons—Tom and Jon are grown, one a college student services professional and the other an aerospace/biomedical engineer. Being a longtime stepdad to both of them has been one of the joys of my life.

Now empty nesters, Jo and I live in our Colfax Avenue house, which we have remodeled and updated as the spirit has moved us. We enjoy each other and good health, ready—we think—for what life will bring us.

Afterword: An Invitation to Fathers

※ ※ ※

When I was a single dad, I worked for pay and was fully responsible for my children's welfare. The same was true of the single moms I met. I thought that we single parents lived very differently than married couples with children. Historically, in my family and most others, dads chiefly worked for pay outside of the home and moms did nearly all the childcare and household jobs. By the 1980s, that societal pattern had changed in Minneapolis and elsewhere. Many married women with children were now working outside of the home, too. What I didn't realize was that most of these moms, while working paid jobs, were also principally responsible for childcare and household duties. They were, in many ways, acting like single parents.

The author Arlie Hochschild named this trend "the second shift." As I got to know more married couples, I saw it in play. While many couples accepted it, and some preferred it, it seemed to me that it often impacted both moms and dads negatively. For working moms, their careers were slowed or possibly limited across their lives. Their agenda inside and outside the home was demanding, even exhausting. Their search for identity could be challenged. One mom—a friend—said to me, "I could make a real difference at my job, but I just don't have the time."

For some dads I've known who had second-shift wives or partners, their work became their lives or close to it—the longer their work hours, the better, they thought. Becoming a workaholic can be the norm and a rewarding one. But they missed important experiences—birthday parties, school events, vacations—with their family members. They sometimes overlooked opportunities for their own growth and development—personally or professionally. One male colleague of mine told me, "I got the job I wanted, and I think I am good at it, but I just can't get away from it."

A lot of factors contribute to the existence of the second shift for married moms. One of the most important ones is how dads define their roles as fathers and partners. Traditional ways of defining their roles are what a lot of dads know. It's the model they saw in their families, the one still prevalent today. I wonder what would happen if more men prioritized being what I call everyday dads.

Being an everyday dad is about three things: fully parenting your kids, sharing family responsibilities equally with your partner, if you have one, and finding balance among work, family, and other commitments. Everyday dads choose to be involved in the activities of their kids and, in positive and recurring ways, build important relationships with them. This means going beyond what are often seen as the fun things—playing at the park, taking kids to movies, for example—and accepting the hard stuff: nursing your sick child at night or dealing with your kid's emotional issues.

I think the most significant challenge for many dads is to equally share family responsibilities with their partners—to commit the time and energy needed to lift what is often a burden of parenting and household roles from them. For most dads, that means respectfully agreeing with their partners on divisions of labor and letting go of at least some work tasks. Not easy things to do.

Becoming an everyday dad requires men to change, as it did for many of us who were single parents. There are trade-offs to accept—less time at work for more time with our children, less emphasis on career growth and more engagement in family life, more development of household skills and less focus on job performance, and more setting of priorities across competing work, family, and sometimes community demands.

I remember how hard it felt to get the basics done at work, and not a lot more, because I needed to go home and take care of the kids and our household. Postponing progress in my advanced degree program, ignoring possible job promotions, and rarely seeking new jobs was a downer for me. I think many men with similar goals will feel the same way that I did.

It is also a challenge to take on household jobs and do them well. Again, as a single parent, I put in a lot of effort learning cooking, cleaning, home repair tasks, care and maintenance of our yard and garage, and so on. I didn't always do as well as I wanted. Everyday dads may not be any more successful than I was, and they have the additional challenge of working with their partners to decide on how to share responsibility for all family roles.

Then there is the connection with our children. Single parents or not, investing more time with them doesn't automatically result in more closeness for them or for us. Setting realistic expectations and working on them is a challenge, too.

What would it be like for couples if more men were everyday dads? Stay-at-home dads and their partners already know the answer. But most men, I believe, want to work for pay in a significant fashion. We have a sense of what the challenges and obstacles are for them. What if large numbers of men brought to fathering the same commitment and attitudes that so many bring to their work? Being fair-minded, a problem solver, a team player. Never missing a day. Working overtime. Taking pride in everything they do. I've seen these qualities in the men I've known—employees, colleagues, family, and friends. Wouldn't this be a game changer? An equally important question is what would be the most likely benefits of being an everyday father for moms, dads, and their children.

We have clues. We know that dads make a positive difference when they are actively involved in the lives of their children. Emerging research documents these and other benefits for kids: more success in school, adult careers, and intimate relationships, and less involvement in crime and self-destructive behaviors. Meaningful outcomes.

What about the benefits for everyday dads themselves and their partners? These aren't typically documented in academic research studies. I asked ten everyday dads—male family members and close friends—a number of questions about the fathering they did in their families. Ten is not a large group, but it's big enough to provide a variety of responses and possibly some patterns.

These men ranged in age from their forties to their eighties. College-educated, one an African American, the others white, they grew up in cities, suburbs, and small towns in Minnesota, Iowa, Wisconsin, Illinois, New York, and California. They come from similar but not uniform backgrounds and experiences. Throughout their lives, they have worked full-time for pay.

These dads have children of all ages, from five to over fifty. They share parenting with their partners. A few coparented when divorced or separated from their partners for short periods of time. The scope of what they shared varied but was usually significant. They faced challenging circumstances in our society: one is in an interracial marriage; one experienced the death of a child; several are members of families with continuing intergenerational conflicts; others have dealt with difficult work, educational, and financial situations. I thought highlighting the perspectives of these dads would offer additional insights into being an everyday father over time.

Below are the four questions I asked this group of dads and summaries of their responses.

How did your experience help you develop your fathering practices? Most of the dads said they learned to father through their experience, a "trial and error" process, in "an evolving way," through "osmosis." Half had grown up spending little or no time living with their dads: one lived in a foster home; most others had divorced parents. With dads largely absent from their lives, there were few fathering behaviors to emulate. They made up their own fathering practices.

The others grew up with their biological fathers. One said his dad "influenced the expectations I had for myself." Some said their parents worked as a team and set clear expectations. One commented, "I have a voice in my head from my parents . . . a guiding compass . . . that helps me make good decisions."

For some respondents, grandfathers, uncles, or family friends served as models, as did current friends who are fathers. One said their grandfathers "made distinctive impressions that pointed how I might act and behave."

How do you think your parenting has benefited your children? All the dads thought they had had a positive impact on their children by "showing up," by "being there," by being "emotionally present" in everyday interactions and ongoing activities with them. These activities ranged from feeding, caring for, and playing with their children to helping with family house-hold chores, supporting them in sports and arts programs, and listening to and communicating with them, especially when they felt their kids needed it. Most were or are regularly home for family dinners and plan and participate in family activities.

They said the sacrifices they made for their kids—in time and money invested—were appreciated, as were their efforts to instill positive values, such as setting fair expectations, being accountable for one's behaviors, and doing one's best. One dad said he's tried to be a good teacher of life skills and values that will help his small kids "launch with a foundation for a happy and successful life . . . build an inner confidence to take chances and follow their dreams." Another dad thought he had modeled the value of hard work, of providing for his family, of being trustworthy, which he later saw in the behaviors of his adult children.

Another dad, who had grown up in a dysfunctional family damaged by alcohol abuse, said he and his wife made it a priority to stop this history from continuing in their marriage for their children's benefit. They didn't abuse alcohol and talked with their kids in "family councils" about how to avoid it. Another, who grew up with an everyday dad, remembered that he and his brother were grateful for their dad's commitment and "knew he cared." He sensed his children felt the same way about him.

How do you think your shared parenting with your partner has benefited her? The dads perceived that their shared parenting was beneficial to their wives. One said the sharing "allowed her to pursue career accomplish-ments that might have been out of reach otherwise" and "affirmed her value and the value of her work." He believes he demonstrated to his kids and his wife that "a man can shape his life in a different way for the sake of facilitating his wife's striving." Another said his wife "thrived being in a loving family, by being successful as a mother and wife and being able to pursue her dreams—pursue her own thing for work."

A third said that his and his wife's parenting styles were similar, with nuanced differences, which benefited them and their child by demonstrat-ing the value of different, shared perspectives. Similarly, another dad said, "We both have primary and shared roles, but, most importantly, we have a sounding board, a partner, and the ability to support each other as times, situations . . . and challenges . . . may dictate." Another dad said, "It is exemplary for kids to see their parents as a team, as a couple, as partners who guide and support everyone in the roost."

Other dads observed that their efforts provided their partners with private time for pursuing their personal interests and friendships as well as professional endeavors.

How do you think your parenting has benefited you? All the dads described their fathering as integral to their identities, to their growth and development, their maturing as men. The following quotes were typical: One said, "Being a father continues to be a great experience. . . . It is the best and most challenging experience I've had. . . . I've learned a bunch and continue to learn more." A second dad said that being a father "is incredibly rewarding. It provides a bigger purpose, but also every day it makes me want to be a better person." A third commented that "parenting redefined my identity as a man—a fuller person, more in touch with my feelings and perspectives. It enabled me, elevated me, enhanced me by increasing my understanding of my relationships with my children and partner and family."

A dad of two daughters said, "Parenting has taught me how to better reach my human potential in relation to others, chart a stable course, and put away matters that as a younger man I was concerned with. . . . It is a special relationship that is unique in life and takes precedence over self-interests." Another mentioned, "My increased measure of my worth as a person is tied to my faithfulness in being a reliable, available, consistent father."

A dad of a son and daughter said, "I would not be the person that I am today had I not been able to be a dad—it has shaped me physically, emotionally, mentally, and spiritually." An older dad said, "I tried to be an involved father. It is a fantastic feeling that all of my children show a great deal of love to me, their mother, and each other. It is a great feeling to be a successful father. It is a successful life."

These dads' responses to my questions were their own perceptions of how they thought their parenting had benefited themselves and others. They included few comments from their children or wives, which could have provided a deeper, more nuanced picture. But positive perceptions are important, the longer held the better. When three-year-old Anne threw her arms around my neck, gave me a big hug, and said, "You are such a good daddy. My daddy," I didn't ask her for an explanation. I had heard enough—I thought I was on the right track. I am sure the dads I surveyed have had similar experiences with their children and partners, which informed their responses to my questions. It is not easy for men to overcome the many obstacles to parenting they experience, but the benefits of doing so—whether documented in large-scale studies or gleaned from my small group responses—seem clear and lasting.

I think that the responses to my questions are promising. They document the benefits of being an everyday father for children, partners, and dads themselves. If true of these fathers, what about a hundred others? Or a thousand? Or far more? I think if dads change, so will family life—for moms on the second shift, for dads looking for meaning beyond their jobs, and for the children to whom both moms and dads give their attention.

My invitation to men who read this book is to continue being, or to become, an everyday father, to reinvent yourself in ways that feel right to you. That may mean continuing to do what you are doing now. It may mean expanding your commitments and activities. It may mean beginning activities that are not now part of your life.

I end this book with five questions for you to consider:

1. How are you doing as a parent for your kids?
2. How are you doing at sharing family responsibilities with your partner?
3. How are you doing finding a balance among your work, family, and other commitments?
4. What in your life do you want to change?
5. What action will you take now?

Acknowledgments

⚹ ⚹ ⚹

I wrote this book in a long start-and-stop process. In the ten-year period of the story, I jotted notes about our family experiences on pieces of paper, envelopes, scraps—whatever was near me when I wanted to recall an activity, a conversation, or a reflection of my own. In some cases, I wrote down whole conversations that I remembered having with family members and others. I made copies of letters I wrote and saved those that others sent me. Over the years, I kept up our family photo albums. I stored most of these materials in boxes in our attic. I thought I might use them to write a story of our lives for Billy and Anne. I wanted them to know more about their mother and the experiences we had shared as a young family. I thought they might be interested and hoped it would be important to them. I wanted to remember our time together, too.

I regretted not knowing more about the lives of my parents and grandparents. Except for a small number of black-and-white photos, I had no documentation about them. Everything I learned had come from conversations. I thought some documentation of our stories—Billy's, Anne's, and mine—might fill in the gaps for them, our grandchildren, and others who might have the same kind of curiosity that I did.

In the 1980s and 1990s, I was too busy working and being a single parent to write a book like this one; all my resource material continued to gather dust in our attic. About twenty years ago, I took a short memoir writing class offered by the Community Education department of the Minneapolis Public Schools. I used information from the notes I saved to describe a few of our activities. Other students in the class encouraged me to continue my writing. With expanding job opportunities, however, I set aside writing anything else.

Two decades passed before I retired and decided to write this book. I participated in a class offered by the Loft Literary Center in Minneapolis, which helped me understand the practice of memoir writing. The instructor and other students also encouraged me to continue writing.

In the past five years, I have read many memoirs to learn as much as I can about the writing styles and insights of authors of this genre. I especially selected books whose authors wrote about the deaths of their spouses and the single parenting experiences that followed. These included *The Year of Magical Thinking* by Joan Didion, *Two Kisses for Maddy: A Memoir of Loss and Love* by Matthew Logelin, recently retitled as *Fatherhood*, and *It's Okay to Laugh (Crying Is Cool, Too)* by Nora McInerny Purmort.

I read memoirs by other single parents: *The Broken Cord*, by Michael Dorris, *Operating Instructions* by Anne Lamott, and *Rattled!: A Memoir*, by Christine Coppa. All these books were terrific reads. I also read books on memoir writing and writing in general by exceptional authors, which I found informative. They were *Bird by Bird: Some Instructions on Writing and Life* by Anne Lamott, *On Writing: A Memoir of the Craft* by Stephen King, and *The Art of Memoir* by Mary Karr.

Over the past five years in which I have been writing and editing this book, family members and friends have consistently supported me. All of my meditation group friends encouraged me to write it and shared ideas about its content with me. Thanks to Joe Meyer, Ron Lang, Carol Dethmers, and Yvonne RB-Banks, whose published story of her single parenting experience following the death of her husband offered helpful insights on single parenting.

Additional thanks to Tom Ramsay and Nancy Goetzinger, who participated in the activities of the Forum, shared their experiences with all of us in the group, and encouraged me to take the Forum course, in which I wrote the thank-you letters to my mom, my dad, and Sue.

Thanks, too, to those men who shared with me responses to my questions on fathering. These were Will Delmont, Todd Butz, David Dyer, Roger Israel, Ron Lang, Joe Meyer, Joe Ott, Bruce King, and David

Booth. Their comments about fatherhood were open, affirming, and inspiring to me.

As I drafted chapters to this book, I shared them with a circle of folks. Roger Israel, Marilyn Israel, Megan Kaplan, and Anna Lowenthal Walsh offered critiques of the entire manuscript or substantial portions of it, for which I am grateful.

I invited friends to hear me read excerpts and provide feedback. Many did. These included Carin Vagle, Nicole Weleczki, Stacy Sams, Maggie Cosgrove, Kassy Nystrom, and Sarah Longacre, all of whom are longtime friends of Anne's. They showed affection for us and for our stories and gave me very helpful, specific suggestions on content and style.

My wife, Jo Beld, provided detailed, incisive criticism of the entire manuscript, consistently raising critical questions about the purpose and direction of the book. She listened patiently to my ideas and offered her own for improving every chapter. She encouraged me to keep going when I felt like stopping or giving up. She came up with the book title, too! I don't think I could have written this book without her help.

Our children Will Delmont, Anne Delmont, Tom Fraatz, and Jon Fraatz, as well as my brother, Jim Delmont, my sister, Laura Delmont, and my granddaughter Paulina Delmont read the edited manuscript or major sections of it and gave me helpful feedback. So too did family members Kathleen Dyer, Cary Lane, Val Hoebel, Brett Hoebel, and Todd Butz, and friends Roger Israel, Ron Lang, Joe Meyer, Carol Dethmers, Tom Ramsay, Nancy Goetzinger, David Booth, Donna Moores, Sara Caugh, Maggie Cosgrove, Nicole Weleczki, Joe Ott, and Kris Ott. Thanks to all.

I am grateful to Beth Wright, who as developmental editor shared keen insights with me about memoir writing, challenged me to take on complex topics, and provided resources on writing practices. She raised innumerable questions about the content and style of this book and fully edited the initial and revised versions of the manuscript. She also managed the production of the book for publication and offered advice on marketing and promotion strategies. She was an invaluable teacher and partner in my effort.

I much appreciated the rigorous, detailed copyediting of Madeleine Vasaly, which improved the style and overall quality of the book, the excellent graphic design work of Jeenee Lee, and the valuable development and maintenance of the book website by Brigitte Parentau.

Thanks, too, to Tony Williamette, Mikayla Finnegan, and their colleagues at Minnehaha Recording Company for preparation of the audiobook for this memoir and for their patient coaching during our recording and editing sessions.

When I started writing this book, I had no idea how much help I would need. I am grateful that so many good folks supported me along the way.

Sources

⋇ ⋇ ⋇

Bond, Michael. *Paddington Bear.* New York: Random House, 1972.

Brown, Margaret Wise. *Goodnight Moon.* New York: Harper Trophy, 1947.

Coppa, Christine. *Rattled!: A Memoir.* New York: Broadway Books, 2009.

Didion, Joan. *The Year of Magical Thinking.* New York: Vintage International, 2005.

Dorris, Michael. *The Broken Cord.* New York: Harper Perennial, 1990.

Dreikurs, Rudolf. *Children: The Challenge.* New York: Hawthorne Books, 1964.

Erikson, Erik. *Childhood and Society.* New York: Norton, 1950.

Grahame, Kenneth. *The Wind in the Willows.* New York: Limited Editions Club, 1940.

Hemingway, Ernest. *A Moveable Feast.* New York: Collier Books, 1964.

Hochschild, Arlie Russell, with Anne Machung. *The Second Shift: Working Families and the Revolution at Home.* New York: Viking, 1989.

Kabat-Zinn, Jon. *Wherever You Go, There You Are: Mindfulness Meditation in Everyday Life.* New York: Hyperion, 1994.

Karr, Mary. *The Art of Memoir.* New York: Harper, 2015.

King, Stephen. *On Writing: A Memoir of the Craft.* New York: Scribner, 2000.

Konigsberg, Ruth Davis. *The Truth About Grief: The Myth of Its Five Stages and the New Science of Loss.* New York: Simon & Schuster, 2011.

Kübler-Ross, Elisabeth. *On Death and Dying.* New York: Collier Books, 1993.

Lamott, Anne. *Bird by Bird: Some Instructions on Writing and Life.* New York: Anchor Books, 2019.

Lamott, Anne. *Operating Instructions: A Journal of My Son's First Year.* New York: Fawcett Columbine, 1993.

Logelin, Matthew. *Two Kisses for Maddy: A Memoir of Loss and Love.* New York: Dey Street, 2011.

McFadden, Michael. *Bachelor Fatherhood: How to Raise and Enjoy Your Children as a Single Parent.* New York: Ace Books, 1974.

Piper, Watty. *The Little Engine That Could.* New York: The Platt & Munk Co., Inc., 1945.

Potter, Beatrix. *The Tale of Peter Rabbit.* New York: Blue Ribbon Press, 1934.

Purmort, Nora McInerny. *It's Okay to Laugh (Crying Is Cool, Too).* New York: Dey Street, 2016.

Sheehy, Gail. *Passages: Predictable Crises of Adult Life.* New York: Dutton, 1976.

Spock, Benjamin. *Baby and Child Care.* London: Bodley Head, 1969.

Williams, Margery. *The Velveteen Rabbit.* New York: George H. Doran Company, 1922.